The
Home-Business
Sourcebook

# THE
# HOME-BUSINESS
## SOURCEBOOK

### EVERYTHING YOU NEED TO KNOW
### ABOUT STARTING AND RUNNING
### A BUSINESS FROM HOME

❖

**Maxye and Lou Henry**

A Roxbury Park Book

LOWELL HOUSE

LOS ANGELES

NTC/Contemporary Publishing Group

**Library of Congress Cataloging-in-Publication Data**

Henry, Lou. 1944–
    Home business sourcebook: everything you need to know
about starting and running a business from home/by Maxye
and Lou Henry.
        p.    cm.
    "Roxbury Park book."
    Includes bibliographical references (p.  and index.
    ISBN 1-56565-973-2 (paper)
    1. Title. III Title: Home business sourcebook.
    HD62.38.H46 1997                          98-20433
    658'041—SC21                              CIP

Published by Lowell House
A division of NTC/Contemporary Publishing Group, Inc.
4255 West Touhy Avenue, Lincolnwood (Chicago), Illinois 60646-1975 U.S.A.

Requests for such permissions should be addressed to:
NTC/Contemporary Publishing Group, Inc.
4255 West Touhy Avenue, Lincolnwood (Chicago), Illinois 60646-1975 U.S.A.

Lowell House books can be purchased at special discounts when ordered in
bulk for premiums and special sales.
Contact Customer Service at the above address.

Managing Director and Publisher: Jack Artenstein
Editor in Chief, Roxbury Park Books: Michael Artenstein
Director of Publishing Services: Rena Copperman
Managing Editor: Lindsey Hay
Interior Design: Robert S. Tinnon
Roxbury Park is an imprint of Lowell House,
A division of NTC/Contemporary Publishing Group, Inc.

Printed and bound in the United States of America

10  9  8  7  6  5  4  3  2

# Contents

*Introduction ix*

*Chapter Four*

### Setting Up Your Work Space    75

*Chapter Five*

### Nurturing Your Customer Base 83

# Introduction

Although most of us have spent our careers as employees working for someone else, in small to medium-sized businesses or large corporations, we've probably all dreamed of having our own business. We've been fascinated by rags-to-riches tales of companies launched on a shoestring and by success stories inbued with good old American entrepreneurial zeal.

Many of our great-grandparents came to America because of the promise that here they could realize their capitalistic dreams. Likewise, we yearn to nurture and channel our own energies and creative ideas; to feel a sense of accomplishment and pride in our endeavors; and to reap, for ourselves and our families, the financial rewards of hard work. And each of us wants to control our own destiny.

In the late 1990s home-based businesses became particularly appealing because they take advantage of space we already have. In addition, the Internal Revenue Service (IRS) has made it possible to claim a percentage of household costs as a business expense, so many home-based businesses can be launched with a relatively small investment.

Lessening commuting time and expense and increasing the time spent with families or in pursuit of other interests are also alluring incentives. For those of us who live in isolated communities, are physically challenged, or are caregivers on whom others are dependent, a home-based business—thanks to telephones, computers, and fax machines—is sometimes the only practical means of providing income.

It's estimated that in 1997, fifty-six million individuals are working from home at least part of the time, legally or otherwise. Some are working as salaried employees (who may work some days in a conventional office and some days at home), drawing a paycheck from a single employer. Some may be independent contractors, doing most of their work at their client's site and using their home office as a base of operations for making appointments. Others operate stand-alone businesses, providing goods or services produced in home offices or workshops.

This trend is likely to continue. Managers of corporations and other businesses have found that paying the salaries and benefit costs of full-time employees is not always cost-effective year-round. If work and services can be outsourced, managers can often save by downsizing the permanent workforce.

About ten thousand home-based businesses nationwide produce incomes that average $55,000 per year, and a high proportion of those businesses are owned by women.

It may sound easy to turn your hobby or leisure interest into a profitable venture, but if you expect to support yourself and your family—and convince the IRS that you are serious about making a profit—you've got to be realistic. Too often people underprice their time or overestimate their ability to handle marketing, purchasing, production, record-keeping, and janitorial services single-handedly. In order to succeed, do as much research and planning for a home-based business as for any other type of business.

But here's the good news: There are plenty of resources that will help you over the rough spots. You're not the first person who's had this drive to do your own thing. Aside from the advice your immediate family, friends, and neighbors might be willing to offer, a myriad of material and consulting know-how are available to help you get started.

In chapter 1, you will consider whether running a home-based business will suit your personality and meet your needs. Is a home-based business appropriate for your neighborhood? Do you have the education and practical experience necessary to launch a business?

Chapter 2 will help you think about your interests and skills and discover what type of business appeals to you. We've provided an overview of businesses that are suited to home-based operation, along with some case histories from the real world.

Chapter 3 will help you lay the groundwork for a home-based business. You will learn about market research, compliance with rules and regulations, and financing. In chapter 4, you'll find tips for arranging a functional work space. Chapter 5 will present an overview of marketing, an ongoing task that is necessary in any business.

You'll note that we are not suggesting ways to work at home or telecommute while collecting a paycheck from an employer; this type of situation doesn't really constitute a home-based business.

Appendix D is a state-by-state list of government resources that are available at low or no cost to help you establish a business, obtain funding, and give ongoing advice and support. Other appendices present sources and examples applicable to particular needs and businesses, and the glossary (Appendix E) may be helpful in translating business publications you read in the course of your research.

Since local and state regulations vary so widely, we cannot attempt to provide the most complete and up-to-date information. Do your homework and save yourself a few headaches. In appendix F we've listed books that we think are particularly helpful.

This book is a decision-making guide and list of resources— a sourcebook that can help you build your home-based business brick by brick.

## CHAPTER ONE

# Is a Home-Based Business Right for You?

Joe Huggins at the Gold Coast Small Business Development Center in Ventura, California, says, "Think *pull*, not *push*." In other words, as an entrepreneur you need to be pulled by a desire to succeed at something you believe in, not pushed out of the corporate world into no-job limbo. Some of the literature on home-based businesses encourages you to turn your back on a bad work situation, such as a boss you don't respect, co-workers you can't stand, lousy working conditions, crime in inner-city office areas, or just plain losing your job when the ax falls.

Granted, there are many reasons for leaving the 9-to-5 rat race: You have a long commute, you don't earn as much money as you think you deserve, or you're burnt out. Be careful! You might be tempted to buy into a get-rich-quick scheme that promises you (and thousands of others) that you and your computer can set the world on fire, if you only invest in a package that might include obsolete software and no support network.

Frustration alone is not a sufficient motivation for starting a business. Your reasons for starting a home-based business should be positive and dynamic. You need to be excited about whatever you hope to accomplish on your own. Starting a business isn't easy; a lot of self-employed people say they've never worked so hard in their lives. If you decide that a home-based business is right for you, you're going to need plenty of drive!

Your motivation, your characteristics, your needs—These are the first things to evaluate when considering whether running a home-based business is right for you. This chapter begins with a self-assessment section that will help you examine your entrepreneurial potential. Next, you will consider if home-based employment is compatible with your family, home, and neighborhood. Sections that summarize the typical advantages and disadvantages of home-based businesses will help you put your conclusions into perspective.

## SELF-ASSESSMENT

### Your Personality

**Your Entrepreneurial Qualities** Take a look at your past, both personal and professional. Do you see evidence that you are self-disciplined? Resourceful? That you show initiative and follow-through? Have you often found yourself, officially or unofficially, in a leadership role? Self-employment requires discipline, resourcefulness, initiative, and the highly developed sense of responsibility that enables completion of a difficult job. As a self-employed person, you must inspire confidence in others. Does your record show that you have entrepreneurial qualities?

**Your Need for Interpersonal Contact** Are you a "people person"? Or do you dislike face-to-face interaction? Think about your need for interpersonal contact and whether self-employment at home would satisfy you. The equation is not as simple as you might imagine; home employment does not necessarily mean more isolation.

If you are a "people person," now isolated in a strictly de-fined desk job that cuts you off from others, a home-based business might be just the thing for you. It could allow you the freedom to attend a daytime exercise class, to chat with clients for a moment before hanging up the phone, or work in your child's classroom once a week. Your home-based business might require you to make sales calls or site visits, actually increasing the amount of time you spend with oth-ers. On the other hand, working at home in another sort of business could mean a decrease in interaction: no one to eat lunch with and few new contacts, most of whom you never meet in person.

If you like working alone, a home-based business may provide the independence that is vital to your mental health. On the other hand, a home-based business might put you so far out of touch with clients or colleagues that personal and professional growth are stymied.

If you decide that a home-based business will not provide the stimulation or solitude you need, consider some creative options before abandoning the dream of self-employment. If you like personal contact and would find working at home isolating, would active membership in a professional orga-nization keep you sane? You might consider yourself a shrinking violet who wants little contact. Would hiring a sales representative or selling by mail solve your problem?

## YOUR NEED FOR INCOME

Will self-employment support you and your family? Be re-alistic about your income requirements, including the in-come needed to maintain your standard of living and pro-vide savings for use in emergencies.

Starting a business might force you to simplify your lifestyle. Perhaps you were considering simplifying in any

❖ BUSINESS INSIGHT ❖

*Home-Based Bulges*

I work at home and I have found that this arrangement has tremendous potential for personal growth, because nobody will notice if you eat as many as twenty lunches per day.

DAVE BARRY
SYNDICATED
HUMOR COLUMNIST
MIAMI, FL

case; many are reflecting on the folly of chasing dollars in order to acquire a greater and greater number of unnecessary possessions. Some of these reflective souls see home employment as a means of cocooning. (*Cocooning* is a buzzword used to describe a return to family- and home-centered living.)

If you plan to improve your economic status, is your proposed business a real money-maker? You'll need to determine how much you can actually earn, and don't forget that you'll have to fund your own benefits, such as health insurance, vacation time, and a retirement plan.

If you are already pensioned, collecting social security, or have income property or investments, you probably won't need to be quite so concerned about your home-based business income. This might be especially true if your venture satisfies other needs, such as the urge for creative expression or to contribute to the community.

When you draw up your balance sheet, you'll probably find you can save some money on commuting expenses, wardrobe, and eating lunch in restaurants. (There are lots of jokes about "homies" spending all day in their bathrobes or even working in the buff, but working in a state of undress might not put you in a particularly businesslike frame of mind!)

## FAMILY ASSESSMENT

Would a home-based business allow you to balance work and family obligations? Can you expect your family to be supportive? Working at home means just that—You are working. Your family and friends can't expect to be able to interrupt unless there's a real emergency.

Don't expect to cope with all-day parenting, just because you are working at home. You may have to hire a baby-sitter or place your young children in day care, unless you can work around nap schedules. The flip side for new mothers is that your client can't see you feeding your infant while you're on the phone!

Will your family actually work in your home-based business? Your children and spouse (and other relatives, such as older parents) can be paid employees. Having a stake in your home-based business may teach your children the importance of working for compensation. Shared effort and shared rewards can be a great way to teach cooperation, a work ethic, and financial responsibility.

## HOME AND NEIGHBORHOOD ASSESSMENT

Is your home really suitable for a home-based business? Do you have a space that you can devote to a home office or workshop? Can you use your garage, at least temporarily? Will the space serve more than one purpose—sometimes as a dining room, guest room, or den? (The IRS insists that the room be devoted exclusively to business in order to be deductible as a business expense; see chapter 3.) Is remodeling or adding on an option?

Are there neighborhood restrictions regarding shop noise, chemical usage, signage, deliveries, traffic, or parking? Complaints from your neighbors may result in your having to close down. In some areas, in-home storage or preparation of food that will be sold isn't legal.

After you choose a business, you will need to assess your home and neighborhood carefully, to see if specific business activities are compatible with your site. Zoning will be discussed in chapter 3. For now, think in generalities: Do you have the space for a home-based business? How would the physical presence of a home-based business affect your family? Is your neighborhood an appropriate area?

---

❖ **BUSINESS INSIGHT** ❖

*Profiting from Family Effort*

My wife has participated as my editor; she's a better writer than I am. She has a sense of humor and has added that to my columns. In real estate, she takes care of the finishing touches; she's more creative with color combinations and that sort of thing.

I think it's wonderful for the family to be able to participate in remodeling projects. My kids see me a lot. We've lived in a series of fixer-uppers and, in spite of the challenges, there's a terrific sense of accomplishment.

AL GORIN
GENERAL CONTRACTOR
THOUSAND OAKS, CA

## ADVANTAGES OF HOME-BASED EMPLOYMENT

Did you ever stop to think of what you could do with the time you waste commuting? Many spend an hour each way, five days a week, riding back and forth to work. Tally that up: 10 hours a week, 4 weeks a month, and in 30 days you've spent—just commuting—the equivalent of a 40-hour week. Furthermore, you probably paid for the car and its upkeep, gas, and insurance. In 10 working years, commuting time comes to 120 weeks, or enough for a sabbatical of 2 years and 4 months.

And while we're at it, how much do you spend on your workaday wardrobe? Unless you wear a uniform, you probably can't wear the same thing every day. But, if you were at home, you could. You might need a few "dress-for-success" outfits for seeing clients. And, if you wanted to jump in the pool or jog around the block, you wouldn't have to change when you went back to work.

If you have a health problem or physical handicap, working in a home-based business may be far more convenient than traditional employment.

For many people, working away from home means not being able to participate in a child's after-school activities. It means not being readily available in case of an emergency or illness. Being home-based can give you peace of mind and your family a greater sense of security.

When you are in your home office, your children are aware of your presence. If they should be doing homework or practicing the piano instead of watching television, you are there to supervise. Once you've established some ground rules about interruptions, you can be available to share the important events of their day.

Even if you are not a full-time caregiver, is there someone you need to check on periodically? Would you like to be available to provide transportation for someone who might otherwise be homebound? Have you had to take valuable time off from work to wait for a repairperson or to take delivery of furniture or appliances? With home-based employment, none of these situations presents a problem. Working at home allows you to structure your hours any way you like, as long as the work gets done. If you are a night owl, you can work during the wee hours and spend more time with your children or mate during the day. If you live on the West Coast, you might want to start your day at 5:30 A.M., to contact clients on the East Coast. When you can arrange your time as you like, you might be surprised at what you can accomplish.

And what if you're having a bad-hair day? Or feeling below par? If you don't have to go out, you could probably get some work done at home. If you worked in an office, you'd probably stay home with your sniffles, leaving your work to pile up on your desk.

Do you have pets that really shouldn't be left alone? With you at home, your pet will probably be happier and less prone to mischief. And think of the advantage of pet proximity for you. Doctors say that stroking a pet relieves high blood pressure and stress.

Your home employment could be a plus for your whole neighborhood. The fact that someone is there during the day can be a deterrent to crime in your area.

Working at home may provide other perks. Build in time for yourself; take breaks and exercise during the day. Walk the dog, stroll through the park, or work out with video aerobics. You'll return to your work refreshed. Keep track of your daily rhythms and learn when you are most creative and energized, then schedule your day accordingly. Save those mindless tasks for your sluggish moments, maybe in midafternoon when you need a cup of tea to get yourself going again.

---

❖ CASE HISTORY ❖

*Customized Scheduling*

In Portland, Oregon, Susan O'Connor handles the content for several Web sites. She tries to keep to a regular routine, and says discipline is what makes it work for her. She's up early in the morning, exercises, watches a half-hour TV news program and eats breakfast before "going to work" in her home office every day at 8:15.

The first order of the day is to set goals. Once that's done, she tries to make all of her initial contacts via telephone, e-mail, or fax, before she gets involved with working on the computer. Susan checks her e-mail intermittently throughout the day to pick up responses and new messages.

Depending on her day's schedule, she takes breaks ranging from a quick 15-minute eat-and-back-to-work lunch (if she's on deadline) to a 35-minute treadmill walk (she admits she hasn't been very disciplined about that lately!). Susan typically saves local errands for after work. The only "danger" with working at home, she's found, is knowing when to stop since she rarely shuts down her computer until 6 or 7 P.M. to begin her "commute" to the kitchen to begin dinner or run that errand.

Although she formerly worked at a large table in the room she uses at the front of her home, Susan recently had a computer desk area and storage units custom-built. At the end of the workday, she shuts all the cabinet doors so everything is out of sight. She tries not to work on weekends.

Like most home-office workers, Susan dresses for comfort—usually shorts, a T-shirt and socks, or lightweight sweats and socks, depending on the weather, of course. One of the advantages she's found in working at home is that she can periodically lie on the floor and do the stretching exercises that keep her from experiencing back strain from sitting at a computer all day. Try that, wearing standard business clothing in a conventional office!

---

## DISADVANTAGES OF HOME-BASED EMPLOYMENT

You may have seen the advertisement for Twining's tea: A woman wearing comfortable-looking clothes is seated at a table holding a mug of tea and talking on the telephone. The copy reads "I work at home, but I'm never alone. Every day my friends and I have afternoon tea over the phone. Friends and Earl Grey. That's my cup of tea."

It's a pretty appealing scene. However, the truth is that working alone can result in being out of touch with the world and a feeling of isolation. After being in a workplace where you may have been surrounded by friendly co-workers, you could miss the camaraderie. To avoid this, schedule teleconferences with a network of colleagues or plan a weekly luncheon get-together to discuss common concerns. Join business and professional groups or participate in chamber of commerce activities. Not only will you learn from the experience of others, but you will spread the word about what your business has to offer and stay in touch with the outside world.

Thankfully, working at home has, for the most part, lost the connotation of not being a "real job." You may encounter some bias, but if you maintain a professional attitude, your clients will treat you just like anyone else with whom they do business. Of course, maintaining professionalism means that your young children don't answer your business phone and that the noise of a child's play doesn't intrude on your conversations.

A major downside of owning your own business is the pressure that comes with being responsible for the whole operation. That's when the safety net of a local professional networking group, such as a Small Business Development Center, can help. Ask for help when you need it, or farm out some of your responsibilities. To some creative spirits, the drudgery of bookkeeping is stupefying and is better left to an accountant. Spending inordinate amounts of time doing chores that you don't handle efficiently is not the best way to utilize your talents.

Another downside of home-based self-employment is the fact that business can be difficult to escape, literally and mentally. Efficient entrepreneurs combine going to the post office or picking up supplies with other errands; they keep careful records of business-related mileage. They carry a notebook or planner with them to the orthodontist's office and do some work while waiting for their kid's appointment. The reality of having business always in mind often results in distraction and stress.

❖ BUSINESS INSIGHT ❖

*Pen for Hire*

I have a bachelor's degree in English, with a major in secondary education. I chose to be a freelance writer because, in the unstable world of publishing, it was the only job from which I could not be fired.

BILL STERMER
FREELANCE WRITER/
PHOTOGRAPHER
CAMARILLO, CA

You'll probably think of other advantages and disadvantages to working at home. Take the time to think seriously about them before deciding to start a home-based business. Discuss ramifications with your family and friends, check local resources, and be honest with yourself. If the prospect of self-employment at home still looks good, go to the next step: considering which business to start and researching the specifics.

## CHAPTER TWO

# What Business?

Choosing a business means finding a field that interests you and in which you're qualified or can become qualified. It also means deciding on a business format. Will your interest in food, for example, prompt you to start a catering business, become an independent contractor who sells cooking equipment, or buy into a food-related franchise? This chapter will outline a number of business ideas related to service, arts and crafts, and sales. It will then describe franchises and outline some of the advantages and pitfalls franchisees face.

## SERVICES

### Professional Services

We're defining professional services as services that require schooling or specialized training and, frequently, licensing or certification of qualification. You are expected to have experience in the field when you offer such a service, and you may have to conform to certain professional standards. Membership in a professional organization promotes your credibility, and also provides an important networking avenue. Professional services include:

- Legal and paralegal services, court reporting
- Accounting, tax preparation, and financial services

- Business consulting
- Secretarial and data entry services
- Editorial services
- Graphic design
- Computer programming
- Architectural design
- Interior design and decoration
- Real estate appraisal and inspection
- Tutoring and teaching—academic, vocational, and avocational

Additional information about selected services follows.

**Secretarial Services**   Equipment for secretarial services can range from a basic word processor to the most sophisticated computer and software, plus fax, copy machine, and transcription equipment. The owner of a secretarial service may be able to conduct much of the business by phone or by using tape-recorded dictation.

**Editorial Services**   The term *editorial service* comprises writing, editing, and proofreading. You are familiar with newspaper and magazine features that are supplied by freelance writers. Freelancers also create books and much of the advertising, catalog copy, user's documentation (such as computer manuals), and corporate material that surrounds us all. To learn more about markets for freelance writers, consult *Writer's Market*, a resource available in the reference section of many public libraries. Consider taking classes in creative and technical writing.

An editor may plan a printed piece, helping to determine its content and style. He or she may work with the writer to develop it. Or, as part of the copyediting process, an editor takes a piece supplied by a writer and ensures that it is grammatically correct and consistent in terms of punctuation and

## ❖ BUSINESS INSIGHT ❖

*Write Your Own Ticket*

I love being completely out of the corporate b.s., having a 40-foot commute down the hall to my work, taking a day off now and then without asking, getting in a few hours of work after the kids go to bed, having something new and different to do all the time.

My advice to aspiring freelance writers:

- Develop a field of expertise and become known for it.
- Always make your deadlines.
- Adhere strictly to word counts.
- Become a better-than-average photographer. You make yourself twice as useful if the magazine doesn't have to send a photographer out with you.
- Give full, one-stop service. An editor wants nothing more than freelancers to whom he can hand off assignments, then know with confidence that they will be done well, and in a timely fashion. Deliver the article and sidebars with no missing information. Deliver slides in slide holders, photos with labels in place. Turn in a computer disk and hard copy, and give tips about handing the material to the art director.

Then begin to anticipate what the publication can use, and make very specific proposals. Instead of saying "I want to do an article about traveling in Michigan," say:

*I propose a 2,000-word article about Michigan travel that will run six pages in your magazine, with a seventh page for two 300-word sidebars. The article will consider six areas of interest for weekend trips. One sidebar will cover the ski resorts of the northern peninsula, and the second will list references about tourism.*

Try to make one bit of research result in several different articles. One project that I wrote as a part of a European press kit became, with a half hour's work, a full article for a U.S. magazine. Articles for trade magazines can often be rewritten for consumer magazines.

Try to establish regular, monthly features or columns that you can depend upon to pay the bills, and then pack other assignments into the free time around them.

BILL STERMER
FREELANCE WRITER/PHOTOGRAPHER
CAMARILLO, CA

usage. Editors often become involved in research and fact-checking, and they should be familiar with typography and the print production process as well as the conventions of standard English. If you are interested in editing, consider taking a copyediting course at a college or university.

Proofreaders check typeset or computer-generated copy against edited manuscript, to ensure that the copy has been set correctly. Proofreaders need to understand editors' marks (sometimes called proofreaders' marks) and be familiar with typographical and page makeup conventions. Again, taking a course is often the best way to learn about this aspect of editorial work.

Editorial services—which provide writing, editing, or proofreading, or all three—have a long history as home-based businesses. Publishers used freelancers long before outsourcing came into vogue, and the availability of fax machines, modems, overnight delivery services, and photocopiers have boosted this cottage industry.

**Teaching and Tutoring** Many retired schoolteachers tutor in their students' homes or through extension classes. The market for teachers extends beyond traditional academics, however. Teaching English as a second language, music, dancing, or art may be the basis of a home-based business. Line dancing, for example, is often taught at local clubs as part of the entertainment. You can go to the students, or they can come to you. Dog obedience and horseback riding present other teaching opportunities.

Etiquette schools teach the social graces to children as well as adults. We've heard of people who teach traveling corporate executives and their wives the protocol of doing business in foreign countries. Another teacher instructs wives of visiting Japanese businessmen how to shop in American supermarkets and even how to prepare the unfamiliar food.

Lecturers and facilitators are teachers who appear at business seminars, booster luncheons, and club meetings. It seems as though everyone's interested in learning, self-improvement, and self-realization. Some municipalities even offer comedy traffic school. If you have a specialty that you can talk about, consider marketing your ability.

❖ CASE HISTORY ❖

*Flavorful Teaching*

**A**nnie Barber was a hotel owner in Denmark and managed one in Italy. Now she teaches adult education cooking classes, which are held in the home economics classroom of the local intermediate school. She plans her menus months in advance, so they can be printed in the class schedule, which the school mails to every home in the community. Students pay $18 per class, plus a lab fee to cover the cost of the food and supplies. Annie also teaches smaller classes in her California home, concentrating on specific topics such as Danish pastry, pasta, and bread baking. She asks students to sign a waiver upon their arrival in the home to avoid problems with food allergies or other complications.

## Construction

Specialists in the many areas of contracting (building and remodeling, landscaping, carpentry, plumbing, electrical work, etc.) often work from a home base. Since they perform their services at their client's site, an office and perhaps a workshop or tool-storage area may be all that's required at home.

Female customers often feel more comfortable having work done in their homes by female contractors. Painting, wallpapering, plumbing, and other home improvement and trade jobs are no longer for men only.

Contractors need accident, injury, and liability insurance, and should also be bonded. Permits are required for some types of work, and many contractors must be licensed.

## Other Services

Here are some additional possibilities for home-based service businesses:

- Research—genealogical or related to marketing, for example
- Art and antique appraisal

❖ BUSINESS INSIGHT ❖

*Why I Chose Contracting*

As a little kid, I loved erector sets; I think building is therapeutic. When I was a teacher, I didn't always know if I was accomplishing anything. But now, as a contractor, at the end of the day I know that I hung that door right. It's tangible.

Advantages? Being able to teach your kids. Being popular with your friends because you can give them advice. People are so oriented toward pushing papers around that they've lost their anchor. Building anchors you. It is so basic.

AL GORIN
GENERAL CONTRACTOR
THOUSAND OAKS, CA

- Photograph and videotape cataloging
- Sales-event management—running estate liquidation or tag sales, for example
- Political-campaign organizing
- Fund-raising
- Entertainment
- Packing and organizing services
- Food-related services
- Lodging
- Caregiving
- Cleaning and maintenance

**Entertainment** Professional actors, models, musicians, and entertainers can work from home, using their telephones for booking jobs and a minimal office for recordkeeping. Or the home-based business can include a practice studio or recording studio for use by other artists.

Magicians, fortune-tellers, celebrity look-alikes—what will be the next rage on the social circuit? In Los Angeles, a popular Japanese gentleman makes spun-sugar creations—dragons, fish, almost anything. He is a street performer in Little Tokyo and hires out for parties. Another Southern Californian is the Reptile Lady. She does children's parties with her cast of snakes and lizards. The kids love her and her act is educational.

**Packing and Organizing Services** Packing services fill a need for busy people who hate the hassles of moving to a new home or office. Home-based companies, many operated by women, specialize in packing up at the old location and unpacking and organizing at the new place. (They don't do the actual moving; another company provides that service.) Many employers are willing to pay for the service as a job-transfer enticement when workers are relocated. The average packing service charges $30 per packer per hour. Packing and unpacking for a one-bedroom apartment runs about $480,

8 hours for 2 packers. Packing and unpacking for a three-
or four-bedroom house may take 30 to 40 packer-hours.
Some services have a 1-packer–3-hour minimum.

Similar to packing services are services that offer closet
and storage organizing, which sometimes includes providing and installing rods and shelving. One service offers shelf
and drawer lining and provides scented papers for lingerie
drawers, fabric for drawers containing silver flatware (to
help the silver resist tarnish), and spongeable pantry lin-
ers. The service can provide compartments for jewelry and
utensil drawers.

Garages are full of garden tools and supplies, sports and
camping equipment, and tools. With the right shelving and
hooks, an organizing service can help customers use garage
space efficiently.

For information on establishing a home-based organizing
service, contact the National Association of Professional Organizers, Austin, Texas, (512) 206-0151.

**Food-Related Services** Weddings, children's birthday parties,
any type of social occasion, and business functions are opportunities to provide planning, food preparation, setup, and
on-site event supervision. Many successful catering businesses are home-based. Food may be cooked in your own
kitchen (regulations permitting), purchased elsewhere, or
prepared on-site.

In addition to food preparation and service, you can supply bartenders, parking attendants, music, entertainment, in-
vitations, decorations, flowers, and favors. Remember, if you
employ anyone other than a family member, you have a responsibility to comply with local, state, and federal requirements. It may be simpler to simply contract out the work.

Mobile catering trucks fill a need for workers who purchase
food to eat at their place of business. Although the greatest
demand is during a relatively short period at lunchtime, cof-
fee breaks and staggered shifts might offer round-the-clock

❖ BUSINESS INSIGHT ❖

*Holiday Decorating*

Here's an idea for people
who enjoy trimming Christmas trees. Offer your holiday decorating services to
local offices, stores, hotels,
and homeowners. You
could sell lights and decorations as a sideline. Your
package would include dis-
assembling everything after
the holiday and packing it
for storage.

opportunities. Community fairs, festivals, and sporting events are additional sites for a mobile food service.

Working couples or single parents are potential customers for make-ahead meals. The hired chef plans menus, shops for groceries, and prepares a week's worth of food in the customer's kitchen. The meals are packaged and frozen for convenient preparation as needed, along with menus and recipes for other dishes—such as salads, breads, or desserts—to round out the meals. Even though the food preparation occurs on-site, the chef's business office can be successfully home-based.

Other food-related businesses provide gift baskets, chocolates molded to order, and care packages for college students.

**Lodging** Taking the concept of a home-based business a bit further, many people have established bed-and-breakfast accommodations in their homes. Large older houses seem ideally suited to this kind of a business, especially if family members don't need all the bedrooms.

Separate entrances for guests, or even separate buildings on your property, will enable you to maintain your privacy and that of your customers.

Aside from deciding if you want paying guests under your own roof, you need to understand that you will work long hours and be constantly on call.

---

❖ CASE HISTORY ❖

*Rosemary Ward, Sitter at Large*

Rosemary, who lives in San Marino, California, has a busy schedule, which includes doll collecting and other interests in the antiques field. She likes to shop and supports her habit with several part-time jobs. During various holidays, she makes deliveries for a local florist. Year-round, she house-sits and baby-sits by the hour or day. People have hired her to spend an afternoon in their home, waiting for an appliance repairperson or a delivery. Rosemary relies on word-of-mouth advertising and referrals and has built up quite a clientele.

---

❖ CASE HISTORY ❖

---

*Salting It Away*

**M**any cooks have a cherished family recipe that they've thought of turning into a money-maker. With us, it was specialty mustards. We decided to branch out from the batches we made for holiday gifts and check into the regulations for making and selling food from our home kitchen.

Well, in Ventura County, California, it just isn't done. Food for sale cannot originate in a household kitchen; it must be from a commercial, health department–inspected kitchen. You could even build a commercial kitchen on your property, but your family couldn't use it. However, if you can rent an approved facility at a church, school, or restaurant, you can legally make your food product there.

After considering the logistics of shipping and shelf life, we decided that mustard might not be easy to mass-market. We experimented with seasoned salt mixes and spice blends, reasoning that dry ingredients in plastic bottles would be less expensive to sell by mail order, and less likely to deteriorate.

One day, upon reading the umpteenth article about health, high blood pressure, and dietary salt reduction, it hit us: Why not come up with a tastier, natural, no-salt seasoning mix? We bought all the brands already on the market and critiqued them: Too much garlic, too much pepper, not fresh-tasting enough. We worked out a few different combinations and had our friends sample and rate them.

Once we had our product, it needed a name. The first one we came up with was Salternative. An attorney made a trademark search for us; unfortunately, the name was already taken. We settled on Substisalt and registered the name.

MAXYE AND LOU HENRY
HOME-BASED ENTREPRENEURS
THOUSAND OAKS, CA

**Tender Loving Care** The most obvious home-based caregiving business is one providing children's day care. Most local areas have strict regulations about the facility and the number of unrelated children who can be cared for; so to start a child-care business, you need a license. Senior citizens, too, are candidates for day-care services, either on your premises or theirs.

Busy people often need someone to groom, feed, and exercise pets. Mobile groomers make house calls in specially outfitted vans. Farriers travel to stables to shoe horses. Veterinarians with mobile clinics visit sick animals at home. Some vets make house calls to euthanize terminally ill an-

❖ CASE HISTORY ❖

*The Artists' Barn Bed and Breakfast*

When they learned the Artists' Barn, a historical landmark in Fillmore, California, was for sale, Alma and Max Gabaldon purchased it for $110,000 and planned to make it their home. But when they learned of plans to spruce up Fillmore and two nearby communities, they decided to open the two-bedroom, 3,500-square-foot structure to the public, as a bed-and-breakfast.

For now, it is only promoted locally, through the Chamber of Commerce and the historical society. Renovations are still under way by Max, who is a building contractor. The Gabaldons intend to keep their full-time jobs; she is a customer service representative for GTE Corp., he has a contracting business.

❖

*The Elms Bed and Breakfast*

When Ted and Jo Panayotoff visited Camden, Maine, in 1994 to take a windjammer cruise, they stayed on to visit the local lighthouses. They ended up buying The Elms Bed and Breakfast.

Their inn has four guest rooms, living quarters on the third floor for the owners, and two additional guest suites in a carriage house on the property.

The Elms is one of 15 bed-and-breakfast homes in Camden, each with its own distinct ambience. "We try to support each other for the good of the whole community and its tourist business," says Ted. "The Elms is traditional—no TVs in the rooms, no hot tub. If that is not what potential guests are looking for, we recommend another facility. We want them to be happy."

Ted admits that the transition to their new venture might have been easier if they'd done some research. However, they've gotten a lot of good tips through membership in the Professional Association of Innkeepers International and from publications such as *Inn Marketing* and *Arizona Bed and Breakfast*, as well as from other local innkeepers.

"It's more work, and more enjoyment, than we expected," Ted continues. "One of us has to be here most of the time, and we do just about everything ourselves—keeping the books, booking reservations, keeping up the landscaping and garden, and fixing breakfast for the guests. We do hire some outside cleaning help during the busy season. Actually, once all the guests are checked in, we can go out in the evenings to have dinner or visit friends, so we do have some free time."

Aside from publicity in the local guidebooks, The Elms has a home page on the internet and an ad, not surprisingly, in *Lighthouse Digest*. "If guests don't know about lighthouses when they get here, they're bound to know something about them when they leave," says Ted.

---

❖ CASE HISTORY ❖

*Keeping His Nose to the Grindstone*

Every weekend, Wayne Montano and his wife, Jan, set up shop at a different California antiques show to repair valuable cut glass and crystal. In 1996, they did fifty-three shows. In addition, his son's fiancée does a one-day show every month, estimating repairs and bringing the damaged pieces to Wayne's home workshop in Phelan, California. After repairs are made, the owners pick up their antiques at the next month's show.

Approximately thirty craftspeople nationwide do similar work. Montano seldom leaves California, although he does attend the yearly convention of a perfume-bottle collectors association which meets alternately in Chicago and near Washington, DC. Montano explains that perfume bottles worth several thousand dollars are well worth repairing.

Until 1981, Montano was an air-traffic controller in Los Angeles. He and his wife had started a small antiques business and frequently took damaged pieces to an established repair shop. When the air-traffic controllers went on strike in 1981, Wayne said good-bye to the stressful career and apprenticed himself to the repair-shop owner. He completed the usual four-year program in two years, and then bought out his teacher's business. He estimates that his equipment is now worth about $60,000, including 350 turn-of-the-century grinding wheels for his specialty, cut-glass repair.

In his home workshop, in addition to repairing glass, Wayne teaches the trade to two or three apprentices each year. Apprentices pay $5,000 and can set up their own businesses for approximately $5,000 worth of basic equipment.

Recently, the Montanos started using a motorhome to travel to the antiques shows. They find that staying on-site in their own RV is more practical and pleasant than renting motel rooms. In 1997, Montano cut back his show schedule and hopes gradually to spend less time on the road and increase the amount of teaching he does.

---

imals, to spare them and their owners the trauma of going to a clinic.

**Cleaning and Maintenance** As "common as dirt" among home-based businesses are cleaning services. With so many women and men working away from home, hiring someone to clean the house is no longer a luxury. Businesses often employ outside cleaning services, rather than employing a full-time cleaning staff.

Although the typical house cleaner works independently, many entrepreneurs employ crews of men and women. A

---

❖ CASE HISTORY ❖

*Crime Scene Steam and Clean*

As the result of a friend's personal tragedy, a suicide in Chicago, Kathie Jo Kadziauskas learned that when investigators leave a crime scene, family, friends, or property owners may be left not only with the trauma of the crime, but also with a horrible cleanup job. The experience led her to discover the niche market for her home-based business.

Kathie serves a five-county area of Southern California, mainly by referrals from law enforcement personnel, whom she contacts regularly, leaving her business card. She is her only full-time employee; if she needs help, she has a pool of workers—mainly nurses, security guards, and police officers—who have full-time jobs but are available to Kathie between shifts.

Kathie has had to develop her own methods and cleaning materials to handle the hazardous substances she must eliminate. She and her crew wear protective clothing, including goggles and facemasks. All her materials must be disposable, even vacuum cleaners.

She uses a time plus labor and materials formula to calculate her fees, and she has found that homeowners' insurance policies usually cover the cost of a crime-scene cleanup.

An offshoot of Kathie's business is that she is now a distributor for an Australian product, ExStink, that reduces odors. She says it has enabled her to salvage property that otherwise would have to be destroyed. Police officers use it to freshen their unwashable bulletproof vests, squad cars, and holding tanks.

As the result of publicity in the *Wall Street Journal* and other publications, Kathie has had inquiries from several states and foreign countries from people who are interested in starting a similar business.

---

crew can clean several homes in a day. They may or may not do windows.

For a household that doesn't require weekly or twice-monthly cleaning, cleaning services may offer a seasonable cleaning schedule. Also, they frequently offer move-out and move-in cleaning.

A friend of ours put himself through college by operating a window-washing service. Other specialties are chimney sweeping and pool maintenance. Snowplowing is a natural in cold-weather areas.

Plant care is another service that businesses hire. The service provider feeds, waters, and replaces plants in offices and stores.

---

❖ CASE HISTORY ❖

---

*Self-employment Was in the Cards*

Our company name is Scott Cards Inc. Located near Los Angeles, we produce everyday greeting cards and wholesale them throughout California. Our designs are also sold nationwide by Recycled Paper Greetings, a major greeting card company based in Chicago. Scott Cards began as a three-person partnership in 1984. In 1986, the company became an S corporation (a business structure that offers some of the protections of a corporation but whose principals pay taxes on profits individually).

Of the three original partners, two had formal art training, all had a strong business background, and one was a former greeting card salesman. Without that background and experience, we would probably not be in business today.

We chose the greeting card field because of our business experience, art talent, and creative urges. We also wanted to work at home and manage our own company.

For the first 8 years, our company was the main source of income for two of the three participants, with part-time income for the third person. Later, because of declining business due to the 1994 Northridge earthquake and subsequent California recession, one participant left the company to pursue other interests. To keep Scott Cards solvent, the two remaining participants drew partial salaries, a practice that continues today. At our present recovery rate, we expect income to return to normal in 1998.

My brother and I run the company and are its only employees. In addition to creating greeting cards for Recycled Paper Greetings, we perform all the business functions, including administration, accounting, payroll, collection, customer relations, packaging, and shipping. Our card lines are sold by independent sales representatives on a commission basis. We have artists under contract who receive royalties for designs that we publish and sell.

HUGH SCOTT
SCOTT CARDS
NEWBURY PARK, CA

---

A mobile car-detailing service tours large office complexes on a regular schedule, washing cars on the spot. The owners leave their car keys with the receptionist in their office, and the detailers collect their fee when they return the keys to the owners.

Since some large pieces of furniture cannot be easily transported for repairs and refinishing, mobile restoration services, such as Furniture Medic, make house calls.

# MANUFACTURING

## Arts and Crafts

Could you sell photographs to publishers? Do you have metalworking skills? Could you offer afghans at a crafts fair? Artistic talent or a craftsperson's skill can serve as the basis for a home-based business enterprise. Consider the following ideas for an arts or crafts business:

- Photography
- Portraiture, sketching
- Stenciling
- Silhouette production
- Calligraphy
- Pottery
- Ceramics

---

### ❖ CASE HISTORY ❖

*Mail Order Plants and Produce*

Mary Ann Spurlock has turned her iris- and avocado-growing talents into a plant and produce business, Rancho de Los Flores, in Somis, California. She sells mainly by mail order, though she also has space at local farmers' markets two days a week. Mary Ann's catalog lists more than 500 varieties of tall, border, intermediate, standard dwarf, miniature tall, and miniature dwarf bearded iris varieties, plus Siberian and arilbred iris, spurias, and daylilies. Iris colors range from white, pink, and pale yellow to bronze, mahogany and dark navy blue, with many blends of two or more colors.

Her 40-acre garden (20 acres in Hass avocados) is open to visitors on weekends in April and May, and by appointment the remainder of the year. She has also developed a hilltop area of the property into an outdoor country setting for weddings and receptions, group picnics, and other special events. It's a year-round operation; most weddings are held between April and October, but during the winter months, the next season's brides come to have a look at the facility and make their arrangements.

Mary Ann does most of the work herself, with the help of her husband. The couple also derives income from rental property. They have one full-time gardener and another part-time person who sometimes handles the farmers' markets.

---

---

*Turning Silver into Gold*

Members of the Society of American Silversmiths, who create and repair sterling holloware, flatware, and sculpture, charge $15 to $80 per hour for their skills. Jeffrey Herman, founder and executive director of the organization, explains: "Silversmiths who are technically proficient and have the ability to aggressively market their work will be in great demand."

Herman, who specializes in silver restoration and conservation, also does product development work and occasionally makes one-of-a-kind pieces in his Providence, Rhode Island, workshop. "Before specializing in an area, being open to the many options that present themselves will put you at a major advantage over your competition. Constantly turning away work without investigating its merits as an income producer is counterproductive," Herman says.

"Silversmithing can be a lifelong career if you listen to your customers' needs and the more general needs of the masses. And, there's nothing more rewarding than creating something with your own two hands."

---

- Stained-glass work
- Jewelry making and repair
- Woodcarving
- Furniture repair
- Textile work—weaving, batiking, quilting, tailoring
- Knitting and crocheting
- Candlemaking
- Flower drying and arranging

## Animals and Plants

Although family farms could probably be considered home-based businesses, even small-scale animal and plant production can be income-producing. Raising purebred dogs and cats, exotic birds and reptiles, pot-bellied pigs, miniature horses, ferrets, guinea pigs and hampsters can often be done for profit.

---

### ❖ CASE HISTORY ❖

*Amelia's Big Bow Business*

Amelia McCoy of Lamar, Oklahoma, made her own hairbows as a child; as an adult she made them for her daughter and granddaughters. Eventually, she sold her bows at craft shows, in beauty shops, and to her granddaughter's dance class members.

In 1979, Amelia, a rancher's wife and full-time homemaker who had never worked outside her home, approached the manager of the local Wal-Mart store. The manager arranged for her to meet with his twelve district managers. Every manager ordered bows for their Christmas promotions. But Amelia only had three dozen on hand! With the help of her daughter, two daughters-in-law, and friends and neighbors, thousands of bows were assembled in two days. That Christmas season, she cleared $1,700 in sales.

Within the next year, she was selling bows in five states. In 1992, Amelia McCoy was named Small Business Person of the Year by the Small Business Administration. In 1994 her company, Rainbows and Halos, was producing more than five million bows annually, sold in such national chains as Wal-Mart, Kroger, and Winn-Dixie.

The company is still a cottage industry; the bows are handmade by 350 to 600 people in the community. On payday they bring the finished bows to Amelia's ranch (now expanded to six buildings housing offices, a warehouse, and shipping and receiving) and have a chance to socialize.

Amelia has learned how to sell and make presentations. Publicity about her SBA award and appearances on TV shows have brought more sales, but word of mouth brings in most orders. The company does not advertise.

Says Amelia, "Obstacles and doubts are necessary for success and growth. Each struggle sharpens your skills and strengthens your courage and endurance. You can either move onward or quit. This is when you know what you're made of."

---

Gardening and plant production are also possibilities, and could even include houseplants grown entirely indoors. Vegetables and herbs, fresh flowers and plants, and dried flowers or decorative arrangements made from them might appeal to gardeners who want to profit from their green-thumb talents.

Again, the IRS has to be convinced that you intend to derive income from your venture. "Gentlemen's farms" that are really only expensive hobbies don't qualify for tax breaks.

---

❖ **CASE HISTORY** ❖

*Spinning Jenny*

Jennifer Whitaker's home-based business is in Great Britain, but it could just as well be in the colonies. She and her husband, Michael, purchased a row of attached 16th-century weavers' cottages in their small village. Their needlework-supply shop occupies the end unit. They turned the two middle units into their home, and the fourth unit on the other end is rented out as a home. When they decided to expand, Jennifer found a commercial building in a distant town. There her shop occupies the first floor, the second floor is more shop space and storage, and the third floor has an apartment where Jenny can stay if she doesn't want to commute between the two locations. Income taxes being as steep as they are in Britain, having a combination residence and business offers a definite tax advantage there.

---

## SALES

Salespeople need a base of operations for telephone or in-person selling. A simple setup at home may serve the purpose with minimum expense.

The Internal Revenue Service (IRS) even cooperates if you have to store inventory somewhere in your house; that space is tax-deductible, even if you are an outside salesperson and (as yet) cannot deduct your home-office ex-

---

❖ **BUSINESS INSIGHT** ❖

*Images Are Everywhere*

If you are a competent photographer, there may be a bigger market for your skill than you think. You know that photographers provide images for books and periodicals. Photographers also do commercial photography for catalogs and advertisements. Many of these assignments do not require elaborate studio facilities. It may be possible to rent a studio for a day if your home setup isn't adequate. Currently popular are outdoor or workplace portraits, rather than studio photography, of families and business executives. Wedding photographers are always sought after, and now the ceremony and the reception may be captured on videotape as well. There's always a photographer on hand at horse and dog shows, to photograph the winners with their trophies and ribbons. Trade shows and conventions are other possible markets.

penses because your work is performed on your customers' premises. (See chapter 3 for new tax legislation.)

Of course, if you sell over the telephone or Internet, or if your clients come to your home, your home-office space and equipment may be allowable tax deductions. Consult the IRS for details.

The type of selling home-based entrepreneurs usually do is called direct selling, or selling directly to the consumer rather than to an intermediary. Almost all direct salespeople are independent contractors and not employees of the company whose products they sell. In the context of sales, to be an independent contractor:

---

### ❖ BUSINESS INSIGHT ❖

*Perils of the Post*

Many self-employed salespeople do business by mail, using the post office or parcel delivery services. If you're thinking of starting such a business, consider what could go wrong and how to prevent problems.

Usually, doing business by mail order has worked well, but there have been a couple of problems. Once I answered an ad in an antiques publication for some pieces of Royal Bayreuth china and sent the asking price. When I got the pieces, they weren't the same scale the seller described, so I tried to return them, and she refused to take them back and give me a refund. There was nothing I could do, but later I sold them for the amount I paid.

Another time I sent the money for some merchandise, but it never came. I found out later through other dealers that the seller, who had a gambling problem, was just pocketing the money and didn't have the merchandise in the first place. She finally paid the money back, over a long period of time.

I once sold some items through the mail, but the buyer said he never got them and wouldn't pay. Tracing the shipment showed that someone at his address had signed for the package. It turned out that they'd had an exchange student who apparently signed for the merchandise and took it home with him. It takes a long time to settle claims like these, and I never ship through the post office because claims take forever.

SONDRA KRUEGER
ANTIQUES DEALER
THOUSAND OAKS, CA

- You must sell your products in the home or in some place other than a retail establishment.
- You must sell on a commission basis, a deposit-commission basis, or for resale.
- Your pay must be related to the number and amount of sales you make, rather than the number of hours you have worked.
- You must have a written contract stating you will not be treated as an employee for federal income tax purposes.
  (Note that the same prerequisites do not apply to independent contractors who do not work in sales.)

Unlike salaried employees, independent contractors must make their own employment and social security tax payments. They must file estimated income tax payments each quarter or pay a penalty.

For income tax purposes, independent contractors must report all their income or profit. These amounts include commissions, bonuses, or percentages received as a prize, award, or gift received in connection with direct selling.

For more information regarding forms, rules, and tax liability, phone the IRS by calling (800) 829-1040. To request IRS Publication 911, *Tax Information for Direct Sellers*, call (800) 829-3676. See also chapter 3, later in this book, for a discussion of tax considerations.

**Direct Sales Organizations** The Direct Selling Association (DSA) is a national trade association, founded in 1910, that represents companies that manufacture and distribute goods and services sold directly to consumers. DSA estimates that more than 5.7 million Americans work in direct sales and that direct selling generates revenues of more than $16 billion a year.

In theory, working with a direct sales organization as an independent contractor has two advantages. First, the organization will provide some training and support (sales aids, the opportunity to network, and the like). Second, the salesperson has a lot of freedom—freedom to set hours, determine strategy, and so on.

Brochures aimed at convincing people to become direct sellers emphasize that success depends only on willingness to work. That may be true, in part. But many factors influence success, such as the number of sellers already selling the same product in the same market, whether demand for the product exists, and if the product is actually worth buying.

A look at a list of DSA members shows the variety of products available through direct selling. Appendix A lists DSA members.

Anyone considering direct sales must carefully evaluate the direct sales organization and its products. Examine the startup investment, training and support offered, pay structure, guarantees, and return policy. Find out what happens if you decide to leave the business. (DSA members agree to repurchase 90 percent of marketable inventory purchased within the last 12 months by salespeople who are working with the company.)

Prudence and lots of information are necessary in making the decision to enter direct selling, because business opportunity fraud abounds. The next section discusses a common fraud, a pyramid scheme (which is illegal). Be sure to know the difference between a pyramid scheme and multilevel marketing, discussed later in this chapter.

**Pyramid Schemes\*** The word *pyramid* in the term *pyramid scheme* refers to a conceptual structure in which many peo-

---

\* Portions of the section about fraud and multilevel marketing are excerpted from material published by the Direct Selling Association or the Direct Selling Education Foundation. The material here is used by permission.

ple (the base of the pyramid) give money to those above them. At each higher level, the number of people decreases.

Why do people at the bottom pay? Many think they are paying for help in starting a small business of their own. In reality, each new participant pays for the chance to advance to the top and profit from payments of others who might join later.

To join, you might have to pay anywhere from a small investment to thousands of dollars. For example, suppose $1,000 buys you a position on the bottom level. Of your money, $500 goes to the person directly above you, and the other $500 goes to the person at the top of the pyramid, the promoter. If all the levels fill up with participants, the promoter will collect $16,000, and you and the others on the bottom level will each be $1,000 poorer. When the promoter has been paid off, his position is removed and the second level becomes the top, or payoff, level. Only then do the 2 people on the second level begin to profit. To pay off these two, 32 empty positions must be added at the bottom; the search for new participants begins.

Each time a level rises to the top, a new level must be added to the bottom, each one twice as large as the one before. If enough new participants join, you and the other 15 players in your level may make it to the top. However, in order for you to collect your payoffs, 512 people would have to be recruited, half of them losing $1,000 each.

Of course, the pyramid may collapse long before you reach the top. For everyone in a pyramid scheme to profit, there would have to be a never-ending supply of new participants.

In reality, the supply of participants is limited, and each new level of participants has less chance of recruiting others and a greater chance of losing money.

Know three things about pyramid schemes:

1. *They are losers.* Pyramiding is based on simple mathematics: Many losers pay a few winners.

2. *They are fraudulent.* Participants in a pyramid scheme are, consciously or unconsciously, deceiving those they recruit. Few would pay to join if the diminishing odds were explained to them.

3. *They are illegal.* There is a real risk that a pyramid operation will be closed down by the officials and the participants subjected to fines and possible arrest.

Why would anyone join a pyramid scheme? Pyramid promoters are masters of group psychology. At recruiting meetings they create a frenzied, enthusiastic atmosphere where group pressure and promises of easy money play upon people's greed and fear of missing a good deal. Thoughtful consideration and questioning are discouraged. It is difficult to resist this kind of appeal unless you recognize that the scheme is rigged against you.

Some pyramid promoters try to make their schemes look like multilevel marketing methods. Multilevel marketing is a lawful and legitimate business method that uses a network of independent distributors to sell consumer products.

To look like a multilevel marketing company, a pyramid scheme takes on a line of products and claims to be in the business of selling them to consumers. However, little or no effort is made to actually market the products. Instead, money is made in typical pyramid fashion, from recruiting. New distributors are pushed to purchase large and costly amounts of inventory when they sign up.

For example, you might have to purchase $1,000 of nearly worthless products in order to become a "distributor." The person who recruited you receives $500 (a 50 percent commission) and $500 goes to the top (to the company, in this case). Notice the similarity to the simple pyramid scheme described earlier.

Most disguised pyramids, however, are not this easy to unmask. Pyramid schemes often choose products that are cheap to produce but have no established market value, such as new miracle products, exotic cures, etc. This makes it difficult to tell whether there is a real consumer market for the products. The best way to avoid a disguised pyramid fraud is to know what to look for in a legitimate income opportunity.

**Multilevel Marketing** Multilevel marketing is a popular way of retailing in which consumer products are sold, not in stores by salesclerks, but by independent business people (distributors), usually in customer's homes.

In a multilevel structure you can build and manage your own sales force by recruiting, motivating, supplying, and training others. Your compensation then includes a percentage of the sales of your entire group as well as earnings on your own sales to retail customers. This opportunity has made multilevel marketing an attractive way of starting a business with comparatively little money.

**Recognizing a Bad Investment** How can you tell the difference between legitimate multilevel marketing and a pyramid scheme? Pyramid schemes seek to make money from you (and quickly). Multilevel marketing companies seek to make money with you as you build your business (and theirs) by selling consumer products. Before you sign up with a company, ask yourself three questions:

1. How much are you required to pay to become a distributor? If the cost is substantial, be careful! The start-up fee in multilevel companies is generally small (usually for a sales kit sold at or below company cost). These companies want to make it easy and inexpensive for you to start selling. Pyramid schemes, on the other hand, make nearly all their profit on signing up new recruits. Therefore, the cost to become a distributor is usually high. Caution:

Pyramids often disguise entry fees as part of the price charged for required purchases of training, computer services, product inventory, etc. These purchases may not even be expensive or "required," but there will be considerable pressure to "take full advantage of the opportunity."

2. Will the company buy back unsold inventory? If you could be stuck with unsold inventory, beware! Legitimate companies that require inventory purchases will usually buy back unsold products if you decide to quit the business. Some state laws require buy-backs amounting to 90 percent of your original cost.

3. Are the company's products sold to consumers? If the answer is no (or not many), stay away! This is a key element. Multilevel marketing (like other methods of retailing) depends on selling to consumers and establishing a market. This requires quality products, competitively priced. Pyramid schemes, on the other hand, are not based on sales to end-users of the product. Profits are made on volume sales to new recruits who buy the products, not because they are useful or attractively priced, but because they must buy them to participate. Inventory purchases should never be more than you can realistically expect to sell.

To protect yourself from a pyramid scheme or any sort of bad investment:

- Take your time. Don't let anyone rush you. A good opportunity to build a business in a multilevel structure will not disappear overnight.
- Ask questions about the

    *Company and its officers*
    *Products*—their cost, fair market value, source of

supply, and potential market in your area
*Start-up fee* (including required purchases)
*Guaranteed buyback* of required purchases
*Average earnings* of active distributors

- Get copies of all available company literature.
- Consult with others who have had experience with the company and its products. Check to see if the products are actually being sold to consumers.
- Investigate and verify all information. Do not assume that official-looking documents are either accurate or complete.

For help in evaluating a company or if you suspect that a company may be an illegal pyramid, see Resources for Investigating Businesses, later in this chapter.

**Examples of Business Opportunity Fraud**  Pyramid schemes are not the only means of bilking investors. Consider a few examples of business opportunity fraud. They might help you avoid a costly mistake.

*Example 1*  A Colorado man paid $20,000 to purchase a business that raised money for nonprofit organizations and schools. He was promised that he could earn a six-figure income and that the business was new to his state. His distributorship included a protected territory for the state plus 25,000 coupon books offering two-for-one savings on popular items. The company, located outside Colorado, promised him complete support and agreed to help him sign up other distributors to work under him. In fact, the opportunity was not new to Colorado: The company had signed distributors who were in direct competition, and the product was not salable. The company was only interested in selling its own distributorships. The man filed a suit for fraud in his state, but it was thrown out; the court said he had to bring suit in the company's state. The man lost his investment and more.

This offer included "too good to be true" claims. In addition, a company can't really sell you a protected territory.

*Example 2* An Iowa investor paid $5,490 for vending machines and an inventory of small toys. The company promised to place the machines in busy locations and guaranteed an annual income of $42,000. In fact, the machines were scattered over 138 miles, in locations that produced few sales and no profit.

Sellers of vending machines, video games, and the like often promise fantastic locations, easy servicing, and competitive pricing. Verify all promises and make sure they are in writing.

*Example 3* A New Jersey man invested $6,000 to become a dealer selling window solar collectors. He was told that the collectors would sell quickly because of their high energy-saving potential and that he could expect a profit of $4,735 on his initial inventory of fifteen units. However, when he attempted to sell the solar units, consumer agencies requested a basis for the energy-saving claims, which the company could not provide. He was unable to sell any units without making illegal claims to consumers.

Such a dilemma can occur in any business opportunity involving products that are supposed to "sell themselves." Claims that you make to customers must be accurate. Check with consumer agencies and specialists to see if the company has sufficient basis for such claims.

**FTC Requirements for Business Opportunity Sellers** A 1979 federal regulation administered by the Federal Trade Commission (FTC) requires sellers of certain business opportunities to provide information to all potential purchasers.

The following list summarizes the information a seller of a business opportunity covered by the FTC rule must supply to you in writing before a contract is signed. Approximately a dozen states have similar disclosure requirements. Although many sales are not covered by these laws, this list is a useful guide to the kind of information you should have in writing before making any investment in a business opportunity. The seller must provide:

1. The business background of the principals of the selling company, including any lawsuits or bankruptcies in which principals were involved.
2. An audited financial statement of the company for the past 3 years. The statement must include operating revenues and a profit and loss statement.
3. A complete description of all initial and future discharges you must pay, as well as all other obligations you may incur.
4. A description of any help the selling company will provide, including training programs, site selection advice, and financial assistance.
5. A description of the conditions under which the contract may be terminated or modified by either party.
6. A list of the names and addresses of others who have purchased business opportunities from the company.
7. Support for any earnings claims, including the percentage of purchasers who have actually achieved the results that are claimed.
8. A description of any restrictions, including restrictions on what and where you must buy and sell.

**Resources for Investigating Businesses** Among the local resources that can help youevaluate a business opportunity are

- Chamber of commerce
- Better Business Bureau
- District attorney's office
- Public library
- Testing laboratories
- Competing businesses

At the state and federal level, you may want to consult

- State attorney general's office
- State prosecutor's office
- Federal Trade Commission, Consumer Fraud Division, (202) 326-2222
- National Fraud Information Center, (800) 876-7060

If you have reason to believe that a company is defrauding business opportunity investors (whether or not you have invested), notify the local district attorney, the local law enforcement agency, and the FTC.

## Franchises

Like direct selling, buying a franchise is a way to reduce risk. Though both direct seller and franchisee (the person who buys a franchise) are self-employed, both get some support from an outside organization. A franchise is not a simple resale arrangement, however. In direct selling, the independent contractor receives, primarily, products to sell. In a franchise, he or she receives rights. The right could be to a name, method, business format, equipment, goods, or reputation.

For both the franchisor (the company that sells the rights) and franchisee, the advantage of franchising is the ability to sell without making a large investment—the franchisor and franchisee share the cost of establishing a new enterprise. The franchisee makes his or her contribution by means of paying a franchise fee, which gives the franchisee one or more of the rights mentioned earlier. To see how significantly franchising can reduce franchisor's start-up costs, compare the growth of The Gap and Wendy's. The Gap operates company-owned stores. Wendy's operates franchises. In 1970 both firms had two outlets. By 1983, The Gap had 487 and Wendy's had 2,716. By using franchise fees as capital, Wendy's could expand very quickly.

For the franchisee, additional advantages include:

- Availability of training (Ethical franchisors provide training and establish an ongoing supportive relationship with franchisees.)
- Ability to see a product or service with a proven track record and established image
- Opportunities to share advertising ideas and expenses with the franchisor

Disadvantages for the franchisee usually involve control. The franchisor may set severe restrictions on methods or decor. For example, the franchisee may have to buy supplies and services from the franchisor or approved suppliers exclusively. Franchisees must sometimes pay ongoing royalties, and a bum marketing scheme launched by the franchisor may have a disastrous effect on a franchisee. Also keep in mind that most franchise agreements are valid for a specific period of time. A franchisor is under no obligation to renew the agreement when the period expires.

For more information about franchising, see relevant publications from the Federal Trade Commission. These publications are available through the U.S. Government Printing Office. Another source of information is the International Franchise Association, 1350 New York Ave. NW, Ste. 900, Washington, DC 20005, (202) 628-8000.

Appendix B, page 107, lists examples of some suitable home-based franchises.

## CHAPTER THREE

# Laying the Groundwork

Once you have chosen a business you'd like to start, it's time to get specific. Do you know enough about your particular business? Or do you need some education? How will you research the potential market? What rules and regulations apply to your business? How will you finance your enterprise, and what business structure will you choose? What are the tax ramifications of starting a home-based business, and what kinds of insurance will you need? This chapter will address these questions.

## EDUCATING YOURSELF

Colleges and universities, vocational schools, and professional groups may be sources of education about the business you want to enter. Home study may also be an option. Study at home via correspondence course is now being called distance education. Students study on their own and mail completed lessons to the school for correction, grading, comment, and guidance.

Distance education courses vary greatly in scope, level, and length. Some consist of a few lessons that require only weeks to complete; others have a hundred or more assignments requiring 3 to 4 years of study.

Many courses provide complete vocational training. Several courses may lead to an academic degree. Avocational and hobby courses are also available. Appendix C presents a list of distance education providers that are accredited by the Distance Education and Training Council (DETC).

If you are planning a business start-up while working for someone else, use your position to train yourself to run a business. If you discreetly study your employer's methods, you might learn procedures that you can later adapt.

## MARKET RESEARCH

Don't let yourself get carried away with your business idea until you've asked some important questions and done some market research.

Is there a genuine need for the product? Will the product you market generate enough income to support you and your business? You'll have to sell a lot of low-priced product or less of a high-priced product. Will your pricing enable you to clear a reasonable profit, beyond the cost of materials, labor, and overhead? (Pricing will be discussed in chapter 5.)

Are there already similar products on the market, and can yours compete? If you make it better or slightly different, can you make your product more appealing? Do you know who your potential customers really are?

How difficult is the production of the product? Are the raw materials and supplies available? Will you need extensive inventory, or can you buy supplies as needed? Is the product legal and safe? Will the product require future service, and is providing service feasible?

Can you expect to finance the development, manufacture, and marketing of the product with the financial resources you can realistically obtain? Will the payback be soon enough to allow you to keep the business going?

Have you considered expanding upon the original product, if it is successful, and developing related products or a line?

Will you need to protect your product with a trademark registration, patent, or copyright? Have you determined that it does not infringe on rights owned by others?

Spend a lot of time at the public library or bookstore and read everything you can find about products similar to yours that are already in the marketplace. Look for estimates of future needs for such products. Study statistical information, consumer characteristics, demographics, and predicted trends. You need to study the competition, sources of supply, and technological developments that might affect the production and sale of your product. Locate trade associations and other sources of information and support.

Interview people and pick their brains. Ask potential consumers if they have plans for using your type of product in the future. Ask experts what they think of your ideas. People love to be asked for advice! Make a prototype of your product and ask for suggestions to make it better or more attractive. Convening a focus group is a good way to get several people to evaluate your ideas and make comments. Even minor aspects, like packaging or color, could make a difference in how your customers will react to your product. What do people like or dislike about similar products already on the market?

## BUSINESS PLANS

You might think that the purpose of a business plan is to present your ideas to a lending institution for loan purposes. It is just as important to develop one as a blueprint for your new business. If possible, study business plans done by similar companies.

---

### ❖ ESTIMATING START-UP COSTS ❖

Here's a list of various expense categories to help you estimate just how much money it will take to start up your new business.

**Monthly Expense Items**
Your salary
Taxes, including social security, *Dues*
Insurance
Interest on loans
Telephone, internet, etc.
Lease (furniture, equipment)
Supplies (stationery, etc.)
Postage, shipping, delivery services
Auto expense (business use)
Purchase of inventory
Maintenance
Legal and other professional fees
Advertising
Dues and subscriptions
Travel and entertainment
Other

**One-Time Start-up Costs**
Decorating and remodeling
Office furniture
Equipment and installation
Supplies (stationery, business cards)
Deposit for telephone, toll-free service
Legal and other professional fees
Licenses and permits
Advertising and promotion
Cash reserve or operating capital
Starting inventory
Other

---

## FINANCING

The Small Business Administration (SBA) has established financial assistance programs to help qualified small-business owners. In addition, certain banks offer the opportunity to obtain financing through SBA loan guarantees. Check with the nearest SBA office for a list of local certified and preferred lenders.

The types of loans available through the SBA include:

- *Section 7(A) loans.* These are basic business loans with maturities of 10 years for working capital and 25 years for real estate. They are made directly by the

---

❖ **GETTING A LOAN** ❖

---

*Steps in Preparing and Securing a Loan\**

1. A detailed description of the business you plan to start. Include product or service, market, start-up costs, equipment, working capital, and inventory.
2. Explain your experience and capabilities and those of your associates.
3. Prepare a financial estimate of your own resources, those of associates, and how much you need to borrow.
4. Project cash flow for the first three years of business. Show how you will use the business to pay back your loan.
5. What collateral can you, your associates, and your family come up with to secure your loan?
6. Review your loan package with a SCORE counselor.
7. Review your loan package with your loan officer. Show your proposal and projections and ask for a direct loan. If turned down, ask to have the bank make the loan under one of SBA's guaranty loan programs.

\*From the Small Business Administration's Service Corps of Retired Executives (SCORE)

---

SBA or through lenders. Amount limits depend on source; collateral and guarantees are required.

- *Basis guaranty business loans.* This type is made by banks or other lenders for purchases and working capital. SBA guarantees up to $500,000; collateral and guarantees are required.
- *Low-documentation loans.* Made by banks and other lenders, these are limited to $100 and require little paperwork
- *Export working-capital loans.* Available for single or multiple transactions and can be used for pre-shipment working capital or post-shipment exposure.
- *Small-guaranty business loans.* SBA's share is limited to $50,000. Interest rates depend on loan amount; lenders may charge more for smaller loans.
- *Rural guaranty business loans.* These loans are available only in designated rural areas.

- *Small-general contractor loans.* These loans finance construction and renovation.
- *Certified development loans (504 loans).* These are geared toward financing property, machinery, and land development.

    The SBA often introduces new loan programs by testing them initially in different parts of the country. Check with the nearest SBA office to see if you qualify for financing under any of the pilot programs under way in your region.

## MANAGEMENT AND TECHNICAL ASSISTANCE

The SBA offers a wide range of programs and services from one-on-one counseling, business planning workshops, and training programs to numerous publications. These resources include:

- *Small Business Development Centers (SBDCs).* A network of locally-based resource centers that provide free comprehensive assistance to small businesses. They are funded and administered by the SBA and the state.

    The program is primarily designed to provide free, confidential, one-to-one counseling to business owners and potential entrepreneurs to assist them in improving their business operations or starting up new business ventures.

    The SBDC can assist small businesses in many different ways:

    One-to-one counseling
    Entrepreneurial workshops on business issues

Use of a business resource library
Networking with other entrepreneurs

Some of the areas of one-to-one technical assistance most requested by SBDC clients are:

Locating sources of financing
Writing a business plan
Developing creative marketing strategies
Improving operations, especially personnel management

The SBDC offers technical assistance in the following areas:

Strategic planning
Market research
Sales management
Personnel management
Profit improvement
Cash-flow management
Financial analysis
Permit information
Business planning
Marketing strategies
Public relations
Management controls
Sources of capital
Financial planning
Business licenses
Patents and trademarks

- *The Small Business Answer Desk.* The telephone number (800) 827-5722 gives you access to a one-stop telephone source for small business information, available from 9:00 A.M.. to 5:00 P.M. EST. Operators can direct callers to appropriate departments, program officers, or a selection of recorded information.

- *SBA On-Line.* Use your internet connection to access http://www.sbaonline.sba.gov. This site offers access to information on SBA programs, field offices, statistics, research, electronic versions of *Small Business Advocate*, and back issues of *Small Business Success*.
- *Service Corps of Retired Executives (SCORE).* SCORE matches retired business executives with owners of start-up companies. SCORE volunteers offer advice about accounting, banking, government procurement, marketing, planning, employee benefits, and more. Call (800) 634-0245 or your local chamber of commerce.
- *Small-business ombudsman.* The SBA Office of Advocacy serves as an ombudsman for small businesses. Contact the nearest regional SBA office or phone (202) 205-6450.

## BUSINESS STRUCTURE

Which business structure will work best for you? The key factors to consider are necessary paperwork, start-up costs, taxes, and personal liability. Typical business structures include:

- *Sole proprietorships.* A sole proprietorship comprises one person or a husband and wife. This is the simplest structure to establish in terms of paperwork. Business taxes for sole proprietorships are lower than those paid by corporations or limited liability companies. Profit and loss are simply included on your individual tax return. However, personal assets can be seized to pay business debts.

- *Partnerships*. This type of structure includes from 2 to 35 people. The paperwork to establish a partnership is only slightly more complicated than that to establish a sole proprietorship. Again, taxes for partnerships tend to be lower than those for corporations or limited liability companies. Partners are responsible for each other's actions and debts, even if they are unaware of them. Personal assets can be seized to pay business debts.
- *Limited liability corporations (LLC)*. For 2 to 35 people or a husband and wife, LLCs require less complicated paperwork than corporations, slightly more than sole

---

❖ **SBDC Workshops** ❖

*Ventura, California, Workshops*

These were offered by the Gold Coast Small Business Development Center, Ventura, California, at weekly intervals during 1997. Most sessions were scheduled weekdays from 1–4 P.M. and were limited to 8–12 participants. These are typical of SBDC Workshops throughout the country.

| | |
|---|---|
| The Basics of Business | Marketing a Small Business |
| Building Your Consulting Practice | Multi-Level Marketing |
| Current Business Trends | Networking |
| Developing Creativity | Selling to the Government |
| Guerrilla Marketing | Setting Up a Home-Based Business |
| How to Obtain Financing | Tax Planning |
| Improve Your Memory | Time Management |
| Marketing on the Internet | Writing a Business Plan |
| Marketing Professional Services | |

proprietorships, and about the same as partnerships. An LLC must pay tax four months after forming and every April 15. Personal assets are protected from business debts. Note: The Business and Professions Code states that certain professionals—such as CPAs, doctors, beauticians, and lawyers—cannot form LLCs. Call (800) 331-8877 for details.

- *Corporations.* From 1 to 35 people may serve as investors or officers, who must be treated as employees. It takes significant paperwork to establish a corporate business. An $800 minimum tax must be paid upon incorporation, again in four months, and every April 15. Personal assets are protected from business debts.

An S corporation, unlike a regular corporation (which is taxed on profits and losses) is taxed much like a partnership. S corporation shareholders report profits and losses on their own returns. For calendar or fiscal years that begin in 1997, the allowable number of shareholders increased from 35 to 75. More shareholders can help if you need a big infusion of capital.

## RULES AND REGULATIONS

### Licensing and Certification

Laws regarding licensing and certification are area-specific and usually differ for white-collar professionals (psychologists, financial planners, or piano teachers, for example) and owners of blue-collar businesses (building contractors or mechanics, for example). Federal, state, county, or municipal laws may apply to your situation; make sure you investigate legal requirements thoroughly.

## Zoning

Home-based businesses may face legal problems stemming from the location of the business and the type of business. The main concern of governing authorities is usually whether a home-based business will cause an objectionable increase in traffic, noise, or fumes in a residential area. Other concerns are the use of signs, and parking for clients who visit you.

If your home is located in a rural environment, there are far fewer legal questions to consider. If you are thinking of manufacturing a food product in an urban environment, chances are you are going to have a lot of legal hurdles to overcome.

There are four main categories of zoning: agricultural, commercial, residential, and industrial. Different restrictions regarding home-based businesses apply to each. In addition, each category is usually broken down into subcategories, such as light industrial or single-family residential.

Zoning laws evolved from English common law and the reasons for them are obvious. Most people would prefer not to live next to a leather tannery, for example, where the fumes would make their home practically unlivable. In the United States there are locations where no zoning laws apply. In Pahrump, Nevada, one of the fastest-growing cities in the West, for example, you might find a gasoline station in the middle of a neighborhood of expensive single-family homes.

In most communities in the United States, a little logic on your part will tell you what sort of business activity is feasible and what is out of the question. If you live in Manhattan, it is not likely that the city is going to permit you to raise sheep. However, if you live in a rural part of Idaho, raising sheep won't even raise an eyebrow. We assume that you are interested in starting a business in your home, so the question is whether you live in a residential or agricultural area.

❖ BUSINESS INSIGHT ❖

*Discretion is the
Better Part of Valor*

We are fully licensed and follow the same regulations that other California business do. Zoning has not been a problem because we perform our work out of the neighbors' sight—the garage door is always closed, we take our shipments to a UPS center rather than having home pickup, and all public contact is conducted by phone.

HUGH SCOTT
SCOTT CARDS
NEWBURY PARK, CA

If you live in a city, the best place to look for zoning information is city hall. City authorities are usually more than happy to answer questions about starting a business, since they are always interested in the taxes that might result. Typically, a city has a zoning map that tells you what is permitted in each part of the city. If you live in an unincorporated area of the state, check with county bureaucrats to get the same information.

Once you know the zoning for your home, you can find out what restrictions, if any, apply. There are federal, state, county, and city laws to consider as well as covenants and restrictions (C&Rs) if you live in a subdivision. Federal laws usually cover what types of products you can manufacture in a home. For example, federal law doesn't permit the manufacture, in a private home, of toys for resale.

### Naming Your Business

No matter what you're selling, your business name is your first opportunity to make an impression on potential customers. Try not to be too specific. Your business may expand; a general name may work better in the long run. We chose Maxye's Pantry instead of Maxye's Mustard because we didn't want to be limited.

Here are some examples of effectively named businesses:

**IndExpert**  a professional indexing service for book publishers

**F-Stock**  a stock photography company

**Garden Memories**  a supplier of dried and preserved flowers

**Sherlock's Antique Lighting** repairer of period lighting fixtures (Sherlock is the proprietor's name and he uses Sherlock Holmes's silhouette on the company logo.)

**Plush Puppy** a dog- and cat-grooming service

**Too Good to Throw Away** an antiques and resale business

**Sunburst Skylights** roofing and skylight installers

**Hello Central** a service that renovates antique telephones

**Spinning Jenny** textiles and needlework supplies from a proprietress named Jennifer

## Trademarks

A trademark is a word, phrase, symbol or design, or combination of elements that identifies and distinguishes the source of goods. A service mark is the same as a trademark except that it identifies and distinguishes the source of a service rather than a product. Normally a mark for goods appears on the product or on its packaging; a service mark usually appears in advertising for the services.

A trademark is different from a copyright or a patent. A copyright protects an original artistic or literary work; a patent protects an invention.

**Rights Through Use and Registration** Trademark rights arise from either actual use of the mark or the registration of the mark in the Patent and Trademark Office (PTO). A registration application states that the applicant has a bona fide intention to use the mark in commerce regulated by the U.S.

Congress. Federal registration is not required to establish rights in a mark nor is it required to begin use of a mark. However, federal registration can secure benefits beyond the rights acquired by use. For example, the owner of a federal registration is presumed to be the owner of the mark for the goods and services specified in the registration and to be entitled to use the mark nationwide.

Note the two related but distinct types of rights in a mark: the right to use and the right to register. Generally, the first party who either uses a mark in commerce or files an application in the PTO has the ultimate right to register that mark. The PTO's authority is limited to determining the right to register. The right to use a mark can be more complicated to determine. This is particularly true when two parties have begun use of the same or similar marks with knowledge of one another and neither has a federal registration. Only a court can render a decision about the right to use. A court can issue an injunction or award damages for infringement.

Unlike copyrights or patents, trademark rights can last indefinitely if the owner continues to use the mark to identify goods. The term of a federal trademark registration is 10 years, with 10-year renewal terms. However, between the 5th and 6th year after the date of initial registration, the registrant must file an affidavit setting forth certain information to keep the registration alive. If no affidavit is filed, the registration is canceled.

**Searches for Conflicting Marks** An applicant is not required to conduct a search for conflicting marks prior to applying with the PTO. However, some people find a search useful. In evaluating an application, an examining attorney conducts a search and notifies the applicant if a conflicting mark is found. The application fee, which covers processing and search costs, will not be refunded even if a conflict is found and the mark cannot be registered.

To determine whether there is a conflict between two marks, the PTO determines whether there would be likelihood of confusion—whether relevant consumers would be likely to associate the goods of one party with those of the other party as a result of the use of the marks. To find a conflict, the marks need not be identical, and the goods and services do not have to be the same.

The PTO does not conduct searches for the public to determine if a conflicting mark is registered or the subject of a pending application. To get this information, you can visit the PTO public search library, in Arlington, Virginia. Another way is to check a patent and trademark depository library, which has CD-ROMs containing the trademark database of registered and pending marks. Finally, either a private search company or an attorney who deals with trademark law can provide registration information.

**Use of Proprietary-Rights Symbols** Anyone who claims rights in a mark may use the trademark symbol, ™, or the service mark designation, ˢᴹ, to alert the public to the claim. To use these designations, registration or a pending application is necessary. The claim may or may not be valid. The registration symbol, ®, may only be used when the mark is registered in the PTO. Omit all symbols in the drawing you submit with your application; the symbols are not considered part of the mark.

## TAX CONSIDERATIONS

### Federal Tax Information

You can get information and help from the Internal Revenue Service (IRS) in several ways. To order free publications and forms, call (800) TAXFORM or (800) 829-3676. You can also

❖ **BUSINESS INSIGHT** ❖

*Putting the Kids to Work*

If your children can help in your home-based business, you can pay them wages for the work they do. To meet IRS requirements, your children must actually perform services and their wages must be reasonable for the type of work. For the tax year 1996, a child did not pay taxes on the first $4,000 of earnings (that figure is scheduled to increase in coming years). This arrangement allows you to divert income out of your higher bracket and into the child's lower bracket.

write to the IRS Forms Distribution Center nearest you; check your income tax package for the address. Your local library or post office may also have the items you need.

For a list of free tax publications, order IRS Publication 910, *Guide to Free Tax Services*. It contains a subject index to the publications and describes other free tax information services, including tax education and assistance programs.

If you have access to a personal computer and modem, you can get many forms and publications electronically. Download publications by accessing the internet address http://www.irs.ustras.gov. See *Quick and Easy Access to Tax Help and Forms*, in your income tax package, for details.

You can call the IRS with tax questions. Check your income tax package or telephone book for the local number or call (800) 829-1040. If you use TTY/TTD equipment, call (800) 829-4059 to ask tax questions or to order forms and publications. See your income tax package for the hours of operation.

Small-business owners and other self-employed individuals can learn about business taxes through the Small Business Tax Education Program (STEP), a unique partnership between the IRS and local organizations. Through workshops or in-depth tax courses, instructors provide training about business start-ups, recordkeeping, business tax returns, self-employment tax issues, and employment taxes.

Some courses are offered free as a community service. Courses given by an educational facility may require fees for materials and tuition. Other courses may require a nominal fee to offset the administrative costs to sponsoring organizations.

Your Business Tax Kit is a free kit of various IRS business tax forms and publications that may be used to prepare and file business tax returns. Besides the forms and publications, the kit includes Publication 454-A, *Your Business Tax Kit Content Sheet*, which can be used to order additional forms and publications that are not included in the kit. To order, call (800) 829-3676 and ask for Your Business Tax Kit.

Other IRS materials you may want to see include:

- Publication 523, *Selling Your Home*
- Publication 534, *Depreciating Property Placed in Service Before 1987*
- Publication 551, *Basis of Assets*
- Publication 583, *Starting a Business and Keeping Records*
- Publication 946, *How to Depreciate Property*
- Form 4562, *Depreciation and Amortization*
- Form 8829, *Expenses for Business Use of Your Home*

### Independent Contractor or Employee?

For federal tax purposes, this is an important question. Worker classification affects how you pay your federal income tax, social security, and Medicare taxes, and how you file your return. Classification affects your eligibility for benefits and your tax responsibilities.

A worker is either an independent contractor or an employee. The classification is determined by relevant facts that fall into three main categories: behavioral control, financial control, and relationship of the parties. In each case, it is very important to consider all the facts—no single fact provides the answer. IRS Publication 1779, Independent Contractor or Employee, presents detailed information.

An independent contractor usually maintains an office, advertises, and undertakes a financial risk. Independent contractors file Schedule C and can deduct certain expenses that an employee cannot.

Generally, an employee is controlled by an employer in ways that a true independent contractor is not. If the employer has the legal right to control how services are performed, the worker is an employee, not an independent contractor.

If you are incorrectly classified as independent contractor, you could be losing out on social security benefits; workers' compensation unemployment benefits; and, in many cases, group insurance (life and health) and retirement benefits.

If you are not sure whether you are an independent contractor or an employee, get Form SS-8, Determination of Employee Work Status for Purposes of Federal Employment Taxes and Income Tax Withholding. The following IRS publications may also be helpful:

- Publication 15-A, *Employer's Supplemental Tax Guide*
- Publication 334, *Small Business Tax Guide*
- Publication 505, *Tax Withholding and Estimated Tax*
- Publication 533, *Self-employment Tax*
- Publication 1779, *Independent Contractor or Employee*

## Tax Deductions for the Home Office

In August 1997 congressional Republicans and the White House compromised during budget deliberations to reach a new agreement about the deductibility of a home office. The compromise is part of the Home Based Business Fairness Act.

According to the compromise, consultants, contractors, and other self-employed workers who do some work at home but provide most services at other sites or see customers elsewhere will be able to deduct the cost of a home office, as long as it is the only office the worker maintains. The new rules will probably be effective by 1999.

Congressional sources estimated that the changes will cost the government about $2.6 billion over the next decade.

For the current tax years, until the proposed changes are implemented, deductions for the use of a home office must meet the following criteria:

You use part of your home exclusively and regularly

1. As the principal place of business for any trade or business in which you engage, *or*
2. As a place of business to meet or deal with patients, clients or customers in the normal course of your trade or business, *or*
3. In connection with your trade or business, if you are using a separate structure that is not attached to your home.

## Exclusive Use

*Exclusive use* means only for business. If you use part of your home as your business office and also use that part for personal purposes, you do not meet the test. The business part of your home can be a room or other separately identifiable space; it is not necessary that the part be marked off by a permanent partition.

**Example** An attorney uses a den to write legal briefs and prepare client tax returns. He also uses the den for personal purposes. He cannot claim a business deduction for using it.
There are two exceptions to the exclusive use test:

1. The use of part of your home for the storage of inventory or product samples, providing that

    a. You keep the inventory for use in your trade or business.
    b. Your trade or business is the wholesale or retail selling of products.
    c. Your home is the only fixed location of your trade or business.

---

### ❖ BUSINESS INSIGHT ❖

---

*Don't Lose Control of Your Inventory*

For many years when I would have stuff left over from a job, I would put it in a box labeled "Plumbing" or "Electrical." I've gone through stuff recently that I've had in boxes for 7 to 9 years and never used because I didn't know I had it. You need to set up a system where you maintain inventory control. The temptation is to go and buy it new instead of rummaging through boxes. If you have material left over when a job is finished, try to get immediate credit or sell at a discount, or take the time to create a system that makes it accessible. Otherwise, you'll just end up giving it away or selling it at a yard sale for 5 cents on the dollar.

I had a pickup truck that I built special cabinets into; I'd pull stuff out at the job site and people would wonder when I was going to stop. You need to carry as much as you can with you when you're remodeling. You can never have too much right on hand; if you don't have it with you, you have to stop and make a supply run, and sometimes even pack up before you can leave the job site.

AL GORIN
GENERAL CONTRACTOR
THOUSAND OAKS, CA

---

    d. You use the storage space on a regular basis.

    e. The space you use is separately identifiable and suitable for storage.

*Example.* A salesman's home is the sole fixed location of his business of selling mechanics' tools at retail. He regularly uses half of his basement for storage of inventory and product samples and sometimes uses it for personal purposes. The expenses for the storage space are deductible even though he does not use this part of his basement exclusively for business.

2. The use of part of your home as a day-care facility.

You can deduct expenses for using part of your home on a regular basis to provide day care if you meet the following requirements:

1. You must provide day care for children, for persons 65 or older, or for persons who are physically or mentally unable to care for themselves.
2. You must have applied for, been granted or be exempt from having a license, certification, registration or approval as a day-care center or as a family or group day-care home under applicable state law.

If you exclusively use part of your home for day care, deduct all the allocable expenses, subject to the deduction limit. If the use of part of your home for a day-care facility is regular, but not exclusive, you must figure what part of available time you actually use it for your business. You may use the area occasionally for personal reasons.

*Example* A day-care provider uses her basement as a day-care facility. Her home totals 3,200 square feet. The basement is 1,600 square feet, or 50 percent of the total area of the home. She uses the basement for day care an average of 12 hours a day, five days a week, for 50 weeks each year. Her family uses the basement during the remaining hours on weekdays, weekends and two full weeks. The business time totals 34.15 percent of the use of the basement, multiplied by the space, 50 percent of the home, so she is allowed to deduct 17.08 percent of her indirect expenses.

## Principal Place of Business

You can have more than one business location, including your home, for a single trade or business. To deduct expenses for the business use of your home, you must determine that it is your principal place of business for that trade or business. The two primary factors are:

1. The relative importance of the activities performed at each business location, *and*
2. The amount of time spent at each location.

If the nature of your business requires that you meet or confer with clients or patients, or requires that you deliver goods or services to a customer, the place where that contact occurs usually determines where the most important activities are performed. If this test does not clearly establish the principal place of business, then the time test is considered. Compare the amount of time spent on business at your home office with the amount of time spent at other locations. In some cases, there may be no principal place of business.

*Example* A self-employed anesthesiologist's only office is a room in her home used regularly and exclusively to contact patients, surgeons and hospitals by telephone; to maintain billing records and patient logs; to prepare for treatments and presentations; to satisfy continuing medical education requirements, and to read medical journals and books. She spends approximately 10–15 hours a week in her home office. She spends another 30–35 hours a week administering anesthesia and postoperative care in three hospitals, none of which provide her with an office.

The essence of the anesthesiologist's practice requires her to treat patients in hospitals. The home office activities, although essential, are less important to her business and take less time than the services performed in the hospitals. The home office is not her principal place of business; therefore, she cannot deduct expenses for the business use of her home.

This example was taken from the IRS publication, *Business Use of Your Home*. Interestingly, it closely parallels the situation of an anesthesiologist who challenged the IRS and lost, but whose case became a rallying point for the home-office tax legislation passed in 1997!

Under these tests, a salesman who makes calls on customers and then delivers the merchandise to them cannot deduct his home-office expenses, but another salesman who takes orders by phone and arranges for UPS to deliver the goods probably can take the deduction.

However, the part of your home you use exclusively and regularly to meet patients or clients does not have to be your principal place of business.

*Example* An attorney works three days a week in her city office, and two days a week in her home office used only for business. She regularly meets clients there. Her home office qualifies for a business deduction because she meets clients there in the normal course of her business.

## Separate Structures

You can deduct expenses for a separate, freestanding structure, such as a studio, garage, or barn, if you use it exclusively and regularly for your business. It does not have to be your principal place of business or a place where you meet clients.

*Example* A florist has a shop in town, and he grows the plants for his shop in a greenhouse behind his home. Since he uses the greenhouse exclusively and regularly in his business, he can deduct the expenses for its use.

Until the new rules go into effect, see IRS Publication 587, *Business Use of Your Home*. Keep abreast of home-office deductibility law as the new regulations coalesce. Research the

---

❖ **BUSINESS INSIGHT** ❖

*Contractors Hammer Together Insurance Plans*

Construction contractors usually protect themselves by transferring risk to subcontractors. A contractor should have a builder's risk policy or an installation policy to cover risks during the course of construction, general liability and umbrella liability, auto and equipment coverage, and crime (theft and vandalism) coverage. Surety bonds may also be required. Workers' compensation costs are likely to make up a hefty percentage of a contractor's insurance premiums.

RON HAYDUK
INSURANCE AGENT
OXNARD, CA

deductibility of the cost of utilities, rent, insurance, furniture, mortgage interest, casualty losses, improvements and repairs, cleaning, security systems, and space used for inventory or client meetings. Also ensure that you know what records the IRS requires you to keep to substantiate your deductions. Be aware that special regulations may apply to day-care providers. And make sure you know what regulations apply if you buy or sell a home used for business.

## INSURANCE

### Property and Liability Insurance

Another critical consideration for the home-based business owner is property and liability insurance. Here's some advice from Pat Borowski of the National Association of Professional Insurance Agents:

For many years, the limited coverage in most homeowner's policies was sufficient for the majority of home businesses that grew out of hobbies. Failure to perform usually resulted simply in the loss of a client's business. If the seamstress's work wasn't satisfactory, her reputation suffered. But these days, the ramifications of insufficient insurance coverage are much more serious.

The home-based businessperson must simply decide whether or not he or she is actually running a business. To take advantage of the tax breaks offered a true business, coverage should protect the function, equipment, and location of the office and equipment.

Borowski gives this example: Although a basic homeowner's policy will cover food spoilage due to a power outage and loss of refrigeration, if someone makes a claim for twelve dozen quiches and the adjustor discovers a catering operation, the claim will very likely be disallowed. Likewise, if there is a loss, equipment actually owned by the business may not be covered under the homeowner's policy.

Relying on a homeowner's policy only works if (1) the business is never audited by the Internal Revenue Service and (2) there is never a loss.

Two insurance options for the owner of a home-based business are a so-called homeowner's Class 2 policy, which is broader than the basic policy and may specify business items covered, and a homeowner's Class 3 policy, which offers the broadest coverage of the property and its contents. Typically, the Class 2 policy has an added endorsement from the insurance carrier to cover some aspects of the home-based business; the Class 3 provides full coverage.

Questions to consider and discuss with your insurance agent are:

- To what extent will clients be present on the property? If they come to you for services or to pick up merchandise, will they actually come into your home? Or is there a separate entrance or meeting space?
- Will you be in possession of property belonging to clients? For example, will you repair expensive jewelry or other valuables?
- Will you warehouse merchandise? Inventory coverage will force you to keep accurate records, which is to your advantage in the long run.
- Would the loss or destruction of the merchandise or service you provide affect your client's livelihood? For example, will you be in possession of financial records, advertising campaign materials, or seasonal merchandise? What would happen if your children destroyed valuable data stored on your home-office computer?

Or if a hacker stole data from your database?

- Will you use your car or truck for business purposes? Insure your vehicle appropriately.
- Where will you be doing business? Will your company fall under multistate jurisdiction?
- Will you sometimes work on the client's site? If so, you may need contractual liability insurance.
- What insurance does your client require? You may have to provide certificates of insurance.
- Could you be accused of slander, libel, or copyright infringement? Make sure to protect yourself with appropriate coverage.

You may benefit by having the same underwriter carry all your policies. If the homeowners', auto, and personal umbrella policies are carried by the same company, claims can probably be settled more efficiently and you may qualify for a multipolicy discount. At the very least, dealing with one agent should make separate companies willing to cooperate in cases of overlapping liability. For example, consider this scenario: Suppose a client walking down your driveway is struck by your car, which is being driven by your teenager. How many insurance policies could be involved?

If you are an employer, you need to consider coverage for any occasional workers in your home-based business, including someone you might hire for child care. And of course, if you have employees, you will have to conform to state workers' compensation regulations.

It is essential to establish that you are an independent contractor and not an employee. Letters of contract should help to establish this, making it clear that you control how a service is performed.

Above all, make sure your insurance agent knows about your home-based business so that he or she can help you purchase adequate coverage.

## Health Insurance*

**Tax Deductions for Health Insurance Payments** Another provision of the Home Based Business Fairness Act, passed August 1997, will allow self-employed workers to deduct 100 percent of the cost of their health insurance premiums by the year 2007. Before passage of the act, the self-employed could deduct only 40 percent of premium cost.

Legislation in 1996 provided for a gradual increase to 80 percent by 2007; the new act speeds up the process and allows for the 100-percent deduction.

Beginning in 1998, the deduction will be 45 percent; in 2000, it goes to 50 percent; in 2002, to 60 percent, and in 2003, to 80 percent (the previous legislation would have allowed only a 50-percent deduction by then). In 2006, the deduction will be 90 percent and in 2007, 100 percent.

U.S. Senator Kit Bond (R, Missouri) chairman of the Senate Committee of Small Business, introduced the bill. In commenting on its passage he said, "It's not perfect by any means, but we have succeeded in clearing a major hurdle by fundamentally acknowledging that it is totally unfair that large corporations can deduct 100 percent of their share of employees' health-care costs, while the self-employed farmer, child-care provider, or truck driver can currently deduct only 40 percent. It should come as no surprise then that 5.1 million of the self-employed—approximately 25 percent—have no health insurance coverage, nor do 1.4 million of their children."

Bond said full deduction by 2007 represents progress, but, "American families have health-care needs right now and

---

* Portions of this section on health insurance were excerpted from *The Insurance Guide for Business Owners*, published by the Health Insurance Association of America.

I very much doubt they can afford to wait 10 years to get sick. We won on full deductibility, but we are not there yet." Bond vowed to continue fighting to speed up the schedule with further legislation.

One of the benefits most employees take for granted is health insurance. Individual coverage can be extremely costly for the home-based businessperson, but there are some lower-priced options. If you belong to a trade or professional organization, you may be able to participate in a group plan. Remember, as discussed earlier in this chapter, to keep abreast of the proportion of health insurance cost that is tax deductible.

If you need to shop for your own coverage, you will probably be assessing small-group plans and private commercial insurance options. Both types are described in the sections that follow.

**Small-Group Health Insurance** This type of insurance usually applies to businesses with 3 to 25 employees, though sometimes businesses with a single employee or up to 100 employees qualify.

In the small-group market, health insurance prices are based mainly upon two factors. The first is the expected cost of medical services in a given geographical area; the second is the projected utilization of services. Insurers usually estimate the probability of an insured using medical services based upon factors such as age, sex, and medical history. These factors influence an insurer's charges to you and your employees. Those individuals who are considered a greater risk will often pay a higher premium. Of course, premiums are also affected by the type of benefit plan chosen.

**Private Commercial Insurance Options** Private options include managed care and fee-for-service programs.

Today, more than 70 percent of Americans who obtain health insurance through their employers are enrolled in some type of managed care plan. Most managed care plans share the following characteristics:

- Arrangements with selected doctors, hospitals, and other providers to furnish a comprehensive set of health-care services
- Explicit standards for the selection of doctors and other health-care providers
- Formal programs for quality assurance and utilization review
- Significant financial incentives for participants to use providers and services associated with the plan

The two most common types of managed care programs are:

- *Health Maintenance Organizations (HMOs)*. HMOs provide, or ensure delivery of, health care in a certain geographic area. In exchange for a set premium, they offer an agreed-on set of basic and supplemental services to a voluntarily enrolled group of people. There are generally no deductibles and no, or minimal, co-payments. The HMO bears the risk if the cost of providing the care exceeds the premium received. Service providers may be directly employed by the HMO or may contract to provide service.
- *Preferred Provider Organizations (PPOs)*. A PPO typically consists of groups of hospitals and providers that contract with employers, insurers, third-party administrators, or others to provide health-care services to covered persons and to accept negotiated fees as payment for those services. The cost of a PPO is lower

than under a fee-for-service plan because providers accept discounted fees.

A fee-for-service program offers health insurance in the traditional form. Fee-for-service plans enable you to choose your own physicians and hospitals. Most of these plans require deductible and coinsurance payments.

Simply put, coverage results from your insurer's paying "reasonable and customary" charges (that is, reasonable in comparison to those of other providers in the same geographic area) for physician and hospital services. Typically, fee-for-service coverage for employer-sponsored health insurance has been characterized by three major features:

- Employers and employees share the premiums.
- Employees have complete freedom to select any medical care provider.
- The insurance company pays the allowable claim.

In the past, fee-for-service coverage did not often include cost-containment provisions, and the major advantage of these plans was the freedom for the consumer to choose providers.

Today, however, many fee-for-service plans also offer a wide variety of cost-containment features, such as the requirement for preadmission certification. These features can hold down costs for both the insurance company and the business owner, as well as encourage consumers to be efficient users of medical services.

**Medical Savings Accounts**  A Medical Savings Account (MSA) is a tax-advantaged personal savings or investment account intended for medical expenses, including health-plan deductibles and copayments.

Self-employed individuals (or their spouses) are eligible to establish an MSA when they carry-high-deductible health care coverage and no other insurance, with some exceptions. A few types of coverage (through insurance or otherwise) are allowed in addition to the high-deductible health care coverage plan, such as coverage for:

- Accidents
- Dental care
- Long-term care
- Insurance for a specified disease or illness
- Insurance related to workers' compensation and other liabilities
- Disability
- Vision coverage
- Medicare supplemental insurance
- Insurance that pays a fixed amount per period of hospitalization

Individuals with net earnings from self-employment qualify as self-employed, including sole proprietors, general partners and 2 percent or more shareholders of S corporations. You may qualify for an MSA as a self-employed individual even if you receive some income as an employee, so long as you have declined to participate in any employer-sponsored health-care coverage plans.

Contributions to MSAs are deductible from your gross earnings for state and federal tax purposes, and can be used tax-free for all qualified medical expenses. And, similar to an Individual Retirement Account (IRA), any balance you don't spend can be rolled over year-to-year tax-free, earning interest.

If, for example, your combined state and federal tax rate is 35 percent, then for every dollar you start with, in the end you have only 65 cents to spend on health care. With an MSA, you will be able to use 100 percent of every dollar you deposit in your MSA (plus interest) for qualified health care. In this example, with an MSA, the government hands you 35 cents per dollar on top of your current health-care budget.

MSAs were created to go hand-in-hand with a high-deductible health care plan so that individuals could pay less in monthly premiums and put the savings, along with additional funds, in a tax-exempt MSA. This allows you to use tax-free dollars to cover routine and minor medical expenses while you satisfy your deductible.

An MSA-eligible plan must have an annual deductible of at least $1,500 and not more than $2,250 for individuals, and at least $3,000 and not more than $4,500 for coverage of more than one person. The out-of-pocket maximum, which includes the plan deductible, must not exceed $3,000 for individuals and $5,500 for coverage of more than one person.

The total amount you may contribute to your MSA per year is 65 percent of the deductible for individuals and 75 percent of the two-party/family deductible. Thus, in most cases you will only have sufficient MSA funds to satisfy a plan deductible once you accumulate savings from the first year to the next, and so on.

As you satisfy your deductible, you can use money from your MSA to pay for services covered by your health-care plan. You can also be reimbursed from your MSA for other health-care services not covered by your plan but deductible from federal income tax or specifically allowed by the MSA law. Such expenses (which do not count toward your health-plan deductible) include:

- Dental
- Chiropractic
- Acupuncture

- Continuation coverage required by federal law, such as COBRA coverage
- Vision
- Psychological
- Long-term-care insurance as defined by the law
- Health plan premiums paid while you receive unemployment compensation

An MSA can help you save for future medical or other uses, or help you save for your retirement, very much like an IRA. Disbursements for future qualified medical expenses will remain tax-free as long as you retain MSA-eligible health coverage. If you withdraw MSA funds for other uses, the disbursements are included in your gross income and used to calculate state and federal taxes. If you change to a non-MSA-eligible plan, you may retain the MSA account (like an IRA). You can then withdraw your funds at any time, but prior to age 65, any nonqualified disbursements are subject to additional 15 percent federal and 10 percent state tax penalties. And all such withdrawals will be subject to federal taxation as part of your gross earnings.

For the time being, only a limited number of MSAs have been made available as part of a nationwide federal pilot program. Some of the provisions may be subject to change pending the issuance of further legislative, regulatory, and IRS guidelines. Consult your insurance agent and tax advisor.

CHAPTER FOUR

# Setting Up Your Work Space

If your previous office was a sterile, cramped cubicle with corporate restrictions on decor, won't it be great to have your at-home space organized and furnished the way you want it? Do you like soothing background music, loud rock, or the recorded nature sounds of birds, whales, and surf? Plants and flowers all over the place? A cat curled up in your lap? It's your space, so surround yourself with whatever inspires you.

In terms of your business needs, a lot depends on what outside facilities you have available in the community, such as a telecenter or a facility such as Kinko's Copies. Obviously, someone living in a rural area will need more equipment at home than someone in an urban setting.

Consider what you'll need in terms of communication equipment and furniture.

## COMMUNICATIONS NEEDS

Telephones, fax machines, photocopiers, and computers are the main elements in business communication today. Consider what you need on-site and what is available through an outside service.

**Telephone Services** A separate phone line for your business is tax deductible. If you need a dedicated line to a fax machine or computer fax, you'll need a third phone line. You may want an answering machine.

Your local telephone company probably offers a wide range of services, such as GTE's Personal Secretary Voice Messaging Service, Smartcall Services, and Foreign Exchange Service. Many people use a call-waiting feature.

Another option is fax-on-demand service, which allows an incoming call to cue the dispatch of a fax from your fax machine. You can program your fax machine to send a capabilities brochure automatically; the caller does not have to wait for you to retrieve your voice mail messages and return the call. A service that provides fax-on-demand service found that 50 percent of calls came in during regular business hours and the other 50 percent were made in the evenings and on weekends.

By all means, answer your business telephone calls in a professional manner. Try to keep the area near your phone free from noise from children, pets, TV and stereo, and outdoor racket. Instruct family members how to answer your business calls, or not to answer them at all.

**Computers, Software, and Internet Access** For most people, a computer is more of a necessity than a luxury. Make use of the many books, catalogs, and salespeople available. Think ahead and purchase enough memory for expansion and upgrades. If you plan to generate brochures or other printed material, invest in a laser printer. Many present-day computers have built-in fax machines and modems.

To protect precious data during a power outage or other catastrophic event, you'll need at least two backup systems, one for power and one for data storage. A low-cost surge protector prevents data loss due to fluctuating currents. A battery backup power supply will protect unsaved data and allow you to work during a power outage. Develop backup procedures to protect your computer files and store backup disks or tapes off-site.

As for software, you can keep practically all your records on a computer. Ledger, balance sheet, time card, inventory, tracking, appointment, and address-book programs are readily available.

Internet access via on-line services such as America On-line or CompuServe will bring the world to your desktop. For the cost of a local phone call you can download free information on virtually any topic and, via e-mail, quickly transmit documents anywhere in the world.

**Equipment, Services, and Facilities for Hire** If you have only occasional need for certain office equipment, consider renting or leasing. Kinko's Copies, Copy Max, Sudden Printing, LaserQuick, Pip Printing, Sir Speedy, and Alpha Graphics offer computers, copy machines, and other equipment.

---

### ❖ BUSINESS INSIGHT ❖

*A Collection of Home Office Solutions*

**The Weilers** Martha Weiler, a freelance magazine writer and editor in Eagle, Idaho, is a "messy desk" person. Her husband, Bill, is also home-based and chronically neat. Martha's office adjoins the master bedroom suite; she can have a messy desk and close the door on it. Bill's desk is out in the open, with everything in its place.

**Hugh Scott** Hugh's home office for his card company has a desktop computer, color printer, copier, and combination fax and answering machine with dedicated phone line. Packing and shipping functions are performed in a garage. Inventory is stored at a commercial self-storage facility, with space that rents for $75 per month.

**Bill Stermer** A freelance writer-photographer in Camarillo, California, Bill's home office contains several filing cabinets, a desk, organizers to handle more than twenty projects at one time, a late-model computer with fax-modem, printer, legal pads, coffeepot, phone plus cordless phone, an answering machine, and professional camera equipment, of course.

Also available are an array of binding, collating, cutting, and folding services and the ability to purchase office supplies. Some of these franchises offer videoconferencing and electronic document distribution.

In our hometown of Thousand Oaks, California, the city council approved plans for a "telecommunity center." The center will house a collection of technological capabilities designed to bring businesses, civic groups, and government agencies closer together.

The California Department of Transportation has attempted to launch several such projects throughout the state, to be paid for almost entirely with state and federal funds. The goal is to reduce automobile traffic by making sophisticated electonics equipment available on a community level for those working at home.

Similar projects are under way in Davis and Chula Vista, California, and Blacksburg, Virginia.

**Mailbox and Delivery Services** Many people are suspicious of businesses with post-office box addresses, and some states require a business to have a street address. One alternative is a mailbox service. Your address is the address of their location plus a "suite number" that is actually a mailbox.

---

### ❖ CASE HISTORY ❖

*Basement Business Gets Loads of Work Done*

**A**fter her twin sons were born, Mary Hurlburt of Cincinnati, Ohio, coproduced *Double Talk*, a newsletter for parents of multiples. After it was launched, Mary put her computer and bulk-mailing permit to further use by doing employee newsletters for local businesses. By this time, she had four preschoolers at home and hampers of diapers and clothes to wash every day, so she set up shop in her basement next to the washer and dryer. It was a private space, warm and cozy. Plus, she could get the laundry done while she was working! Mary is also the coauthor of the book *Keys to Parenting Twins*.

### ❖ HOME OFFICE DECOR ❖

*Functional Furniture*

Some furniture manufacturers that have developed whole lines specifically for home offices are:

Bassett Furniture Industries, Inc.
PO Box 626
Bassett, VA 24055
(540) 629-6330

Broyhill Furniture Industries, Inc.
One Broyhill Park
Lenoir, NC 28633
(800) 327-6944

Drexel Heritage Furnishings, Inc.
101 N. Main St.
Drexel, NC 28619-3000
(800) 447-4700

Dimension Storage Systems
533 Stone Rd., Unit D
Benicia, CA 94510
(800) 225-3772

Ethan Allen
Ethan Allen Dr.
PO Box 1966
Danbury, CT 06813-1966
(203) 743-8000

Hekman Furniture Co.
1400 Buchanan S.W.
Grand Rapids, MI 49507
(616) 452-1411

Herman Miller, Inc.
8500 Byron Rd.
Zeeland, MI 49464
(800) 646-4400

Sligh Furniture Co.
1201 Industrial Ave.
Holland, MI 49423
(800) 377-6167

Steelcase Inc.
3528 Lousma Dr. S.E.
Wyoming, MI 49548
(800) TURNSTONE

Techline
500 S. Division St.
Waunakee, WI 53597
(608) 849-4181

Thomasville Furniture Industries Inc.
PO Box 339
Thomasville, NC 27361
(910) 472-4000

You may need to set up an account with a shipping or delivery service. United Parcel Service (UPS) and other services will deliver to your door, but if you want the driver to come to your home for pickups, you have to establish an account. For a flat rate UPS will come to your business five days a week, or you can arrange for a pickup only when you need it. Check into special postal services such as priority mail, which many business owners consider a bargain.

## FURNITURE

Don't skimp on filing or inventory capacity. If you have an organized system, you'll be more apt to file papers or inventory right away so you can retrieve items when they're needed.

If you are going to spend a lot of time at your desk, invest in a really comfortable chair, and set up appropriate lighting. Ergonomics are important, especially if you are using a computer.

Office furniture is available at several price levels. Manufacturers such as Ethan Allen produce high-ticket desks, file cabinets, bookshelves, computer workstations, and office chairs. Plummers, a retailer of moderately priced fur-

---

❖ ECOLOGY PAYS ❖

*Recycling Opportunities*

Our community gives us a reduced trash-collection rate for recycling our junk mail, newspapers, metal, glass, and plastic. If yours does the same, you can cut your costs and help the environment. Many of your customers will appreciate your use of recycled paper and other materials, which you can label as recycled. To produce packing material, get a paper shredder and reuse paper that would otherwise end up in the landfill.

niture, offers modular desk frames with add-on components starting at $169. Unfinished furniture outlets offer desks, computer stands, filing systems, and shelving.

If you are budget-conscious and can get by with used furniture, a recent Los Angeles newspaper ad indicates the savings you can realize.

Two-drawer letter file cabinet: new, $199; used $29.95. Steelcase 9000 U-shape desks: new, $2,600; used, $488. Steelcase 30- by 60-inch double-pad desks: new, $1,000; used $98.00. Four-drawer oak file cabinets with lock: new, $400; used, $169.95.

## CHAPTER FIVE

# Nurturing Your Customer Base

Once your home business is launched, you need to continue to gain new customers and keep the old ones. You have to be flexible and adapt to changing conditions and trends. Getting started is one thing—now you need staying power.

## MARKETING

Think of marketing as anything involved with building and maintaining your customer base. Everything you present to the public, from your business card to packaging, is a chance to make an impression. No matter now attractive your product itself may be, poor presentation can have a negative effect. So whatever means of marketing you undertake—be it telemarketing, a press release, or a radio ad—do it well. Remember, too, that the impression you create as the business owner will affect the credibility of your business. In your dealings with customers and potential customers, emanate professionalism by means of your dress, speech, and behavior.

Be creative in considering how you can use advertising, publicity, and incentives. Remember the option of fusion marketing—that is, collaborating with a business compatible with yours to nurture customers. Collaborating businesses share the marketing costs.

---

❖ BUSINESS INSIGHT ❖

*Don't Trust Your Spellchecker*

SPELLBOUND

*I have a spelling checker,*
*    It came with my PC.*
*It plainly marks for my revue,*
*    Mistakes I cannot sea.*
*I've run this poem threw it,*
*    I'm sure your pleased to no,*
*It's letter perfect in it's weigh.*
*My checker tolled me sew.*

This poem illustrates why you shouldn't trust your spellchecker implicitly! Always ask somebody else to proofread your advertising and promotional material before you have it printed. Even if you are good at spelling and composition, any writer will tell you that you don't catch mistakes in your own writing, because you see what is supposed to be in the copy, not what's really there.

---

### Advertising

Say "advertising" and most people picture a display ad in a magazine or newspaper. Don't overlook advertising venues that are less obvious. Would a classified ad in the newspaper be less expensive and more effective than a display ad? Are there business directories in your area that would target your customers? Would an ad in the Yellow Pages work for you? How about telemarketing? Many companies find that establishing a home page on the Internet is worthwhile. A company called Marketing on Hold can help you present an advertising message to those who call you on the telephone. (For information about Marketing on Hold, phone (800) 811-8282.) Or send direct-mail brochures to a list of prospects. You may choose to hire an advertising agency to help you place and produce advertising.

---

❖ BUSINESS INSIGHT ❖

*Spreading the Word*

When I first started out as a handyman, I thought that distributing flyers door-to-door was kind of beneath me, but I did it anyway, whenever I had some free time in a new neighborhood, and I always got at least a few calls right away. Aside from flyers and customer referrals, some communities have referral services. You can also advertise in the local paper.

One day I was looking at property with a friend in real estate, and he said, "You should write about your ideas. Start a newsletter." I did, and I think I had maybe six or seven subscribers. But then I submitted the material to a few newspapers. *The Daily Commerce*, a Los Angeles real-estate publication, hired me as a columnist. Once I had a track record, I got into the *Sacramento Bee* and the *Ventura County Star,* maybe seven or eight papers at my zenith.

When I was actively writing for newspapers, I would be asked to speak to lawyers', contractors', and homeowners' associations.

AL GORIN
GENERAL CONTRACTOR
THOUSAND OAKS, CA

---

At the very least, distribute flyers door-to-door. (Distribution might be a good job for the kids.) Remember that putting anything in a mailbox is illegal. Landscapers in our area put flyers in plastic bags weighted with gravel inside and leave them on doorsteps.

## Publicity

In the context of your business, generating publicity means letting potential customers know your business exists and establishing credibility for you and your product or service. The goal of publicity is less focused than that of advertising. The purpose of publicity is to introduce or remind people of your enterprise, with the hope of gaining future sales. Its purpose is not necessarily to sell a specific product immediately.

---

## ❖ BUSINESS INSIGHT ❖

---

### Writing That Works

Press releases and newspaper articles that you hope to see in print should follow the following format:

- Include date of release; "good until" date, if applicable; or suggested period for publication. (Indicate, for example, if the item is appropriate for a particular holiday or season.) Remember to allow plenty of lead time; magazine editors frequently work three to four months ahead of the publication date, or up to a year on holiday material.
- Answer the basic questions of newspaper reporting: Who? What? Where? When? Why? How?
- List the contact person and phone number; note whether that phone number is to be released to the public or is just for media followup.
- If you do not include photographs, indicate whether they are available. State the format of the images (35mm prints, color slides, black-and-white prints, etc.).
- Material should be typewritten, double-spaced, and printed with a letter-quality printer; busy editors would rather put material into their printing system by using an optical scanner than by retyping it. Or perhaps the editor would prefer receiving a computer disk along with the printed version. Find out before submitting material. If you send a disk, note on the label what software was used to create the text.

The quality of your submission is important. Copy that looks professional and well thought out has a better chance of being published. Include your business card.

---

Word of mouth is one of the most valuable forms of publicity. Think of how many people in your community you already know. Talk about your business whenever you get the chance. Encourage your customers to refer you to others. To encourage word of mouth, consider offering an incentive, such as a discount to current customers who refer new customers to you.

Publicity can take the form of a thank-you note or holiday greeting that will remind past customers that they need you. In regard to holiday greetings, consider a yearly contact that does not coincide with the Christmas and Hanukkah season. Your greeting will stand out from the crowd.

Volunteer work in the community can generate publicity. Consider donating your product or service to a charity fund-raiser. Underwrite a program segment on a public radio station.

Send informational articles and press releases to appropriate publications. To local newspapers, send letters to the editor about issues that affect you as an entrepreneur. Publish your own newsletter. If your town has public-access television, find out if you can make a presentation.

Look for opportunities to give demonstrations, workshops, or classes. Use trade shows and expositions to present your product or service. Civic groups always need speakers; volunteer to speak if the interests of your business and those of the group coincide. Use visuals when you speak. If you are a contractor or interior decorator, for example, have before and after photos on hand to show the difference your services made.

Be alert to the possibilities that public appearances offer. If you are teaching a crafts class, can you realize extra revenue by selling craft supplies? Does a speaking engagement present a chance to distribute your newsletter or sell a book you've written?

## Incentives

An incentive is an inducement to buy. An incentive can be a direct inducement, such as a discount or coupon offer. Offering a toll-free number can be an indirect inducement: You offer a potential customer the chance to interact with you, at no cost. Toll-free numbers that cover limited areas are available; call your telephone company for details.

❖ **BUSINESS INSIGHT** ❖

*Thirty-two Uses
for Desktop Publishing*

- *Marketing* Postcard mailers, customized letters, flyers, sale sheets, brochures, catalogs, posters, advertisements, point-of-purchase materials, presentation folders, customized proposals.
- *Operations* Order forms, price lists, internal business forms, invoices, purchase orders, stationery, mailing labels, reports.
- *Retail* Clothing tags, restaurant menus, table cards, how-to-use or care instructions.
- *Manufacturing* Price lists, product labels, packaging.
- *Service businesses* Instructional materials.
- *Publishing* Books, magazines, manuals, directories, newsletters.

## ❖ EXAMPLE 1 ❖

*Pricing Primer, Greeting Cards*

Our card prices are determined solely by the marketplace. Production costs are strictly controlled to provide a satisfactory profit margin. Presently, despite heavy competition by Hallmark, a retail price of $1.75 per card seems to be holding up well. Our wholesale price is 50 percent of retail—or approximately 87 cents per card. After deducting costs for printing (10 cents), envelope (2 cents), sales commission (18 cents), royalties, credit returns, and bad debt, we realize roughly 50 cents gross profit for each card sold.

HUGH SCOTT
SCOTT CARDS
NEWBURY PARK, CA

## ❖ EXAMPLE 2 ❖

*Pricing for Writing and Photography*

I set my fees by deciding what I want my annual income to be. For example, if I wish to earn $50,000, I'll need to earn about $1,000 per week, or $200 per day. This is a ballpark figure. Short, intense assignments should be charged at a higher rate; long leisurely ones can be charged at a lower rate, as you expect to work on other projects simultaneously.

When I'm given an assignment, I estimate the time it will take me and estimate price accordingly. Be sure to establish if there is anything unusual about the assignment such as travel (charge more), long hours (charge more) or tight deadlines (charge more). Charge more if you're providing pictures and words. And of course, always arrive at the understanding that the company will reimburse you for all customary and reasonable expenses. Always provide a detailed list of same, with receipts.

Finally, price can be subject to how badly I want the assignment. If it's going to be dull and tedious and there are other things I'd rather do, the price goes up. If it's going to be enjoyable and adventurous, I'll accept less rather than risk losing it.

BILL STERMER
FREELANCE WRITER/PHOTOGRAPHER
CAMARILLO, CA

---

### ❖ EXAMPLE 3 ❖

*Contractor's Prices Plucked from Thin Air*

When I was starting out, and not very experienced, I'd have to call my system PFA, as in Plucked From Air. I would stand there, punch my calculator, and then pick a figure. If the customer agreed, that was the price. Some contractors will go to the customer, hat in hand, and say, "It cost more to do the job than I estimated. Can you pay more?" But I never did that.

Somebody sent in a good story after I wrote about this in one of my newspaper columns:

CONTRACTOR: That job didn't work out too well for me. Could you up the ante a bit?

CUSTOMER: How long have you been in business?

CONTRACTOR: Oh, about fifteen years.

CUSTOMER: So sometimes jobs have worked out better, sometimes worse, right?

CONTRACTOR: Sure.

CUSTOMER: Okay, give me the names of three people you gave money back to, and I'll not only pay you the additional amount, but I'll increase it by 20 percent.

CONTRACTOR: Give money back? I never did that.

CUSTOMER: Then don't ask me for money when the job goes against you.

AL GORIN
GENERAL CONTRACTOR
THOUSAND OAKS, CA

---

## PRICING

How much is your product or service worth? What will people actually pay? To arrive at a price, many business owners begin with this formula:

$$\text{direct costs} + \text{overhead} + \text{profit} = \text{selling price}$$

Direct costs include the materials or expenses you incur producing your product or service. Overhead is the cost of doing business: the cost of equipment, supplies, advertising and marketing, and administration. Some businesspeople multiply their hourly wage by 2 or 3 to cover overhead. Your business, area, and needs as well as the season and cur-

### ❖ EXAMPLE 4 ❖

*Throwing Away the Antiques Price Book*

Some dealers go by the book in setting prices, no matter what they paid. I go by what I paid for it and what I think it's worth, within reason. Sometimes it's worthwhile to pay more for an unusual piece, even if it might not sell that fast.

SONDRA KRUEGER
ANTIQUES DEALER
THOUSAND OAKS, CA

## ❖ BUSINESS INSIGHT ❖

*Blueprint for a Card Company*

Home-based greeting card businesses should always involve one or more artists. But first, before trying to get more artists besides yourself, try to sell your designs to a major card company. Refer to the latest *Writers' Market* and *Artists' Market* reference books for company names, addresses, and submission standards. If your work proves popular, then forget about home-based sales. Instead, spend your time creating new designs and cashing royalty checks.

If you insist on home-based sales, first build up an inventory of handcrafted cards, 100 designs minimum. Stick to everyday designs (birthday and sentiments, no seasonal cards). Target women: They buy 85 percent of all greeting cards. Humor sells. So do loving sentiments. Although artwork is important, a good message is the key to a best-selling card.

Your sample cards should be 5 × 7 inches, the standard size, and constructed from card stock. Make them look as finished as possible. Show all 100 designs to friends and family and have them pick the ones they like and don't like. The more critics, the better.

If you get a positive response, prepare a business plan by first visiting a variety of card stores to determine what price your designs will sell for. Follow that up with a survey of printers to determine production costs. Ask how much for a minimum run (usually 1,000 cards per design, based on 100 sheets of card stock, 10 designs per sheet). Be wary of printing large amounts to lower the unit cost; doing so could leave your garage stuffed with unsold designs, a fate that befalls many beginners in this business.

If production costs will allow you to make a reasonable profit at card prices equal or below the competitions' prices, then finish your business plan and obtain financing, at least $5,000. Rather than borrow money, if that is necessary, set up a credit line in case you later decide to abandon the endeavor.

Next, take the best thirty designs and show them to store owners and managers who sell stationery products. Ask them if they would like to carry your cards on a trial basis. Have an order sheet ready in case they say yes. Do not offer to supply a card rack, since most buyers will order less than thirty designs and display them on existing wall racks. As for credit, insist on payment in thirty days—that is, "net thirty" credit terms.

Up to this point, you have only invested your time. If the sales orders don't justify printing at least twenty designs, then stop the endeavor and try something else. If the orders do allow printing twenty designs or more, then get a fictitious business name, open a checking account, deposit the necessary start-up funds (or borrow on the credit line), and print the designs. Stick to twenty cards, even if printing thirty seems justified. Later, if business looks good, you can print additional new designs when inventories run low. Down the road you will need a computer, printer, forms, fax machine, sales reps, etc., but that should all fall into place if you follow your business plan and do things in a careful, organized manner.

HUGH SCOTT
SCOTT CARDS
NEWBURY PARK, CA

rent events affect the size of the profit the market will allow. The best way to see how these factors interact is to look at a number of examples from different businesses.

The examples show that pricing factors are sometimes very personal. Don't overlook pricing conventions that apply to your specific business, however. For example, craftspeople may sell their wares for less when selling from their home rather than at shows. The lower price is called the home price, which may be 20 percent less than the show price. A kit—components and instructions in a plastic bag with a header card—usually retail for four times the cost of the materials. If you don't know about pricing conventions in your business, you may find that your pricing decisions have rendered your product or service noncompetitive.

Decision making and implementation: These are the challenging tasks that never end for a self-employed person. From assessing yourself to assessing the market, from financing to advertising, every step requires active involvement and presents the opportunity for tremendous satisfaction. As you read the business insight on page 90, notice all the decisions the business owner faces and project their ramifications for financing, marketing, pricing—and, of course, profits.

# Direct Selling Association Members

The list that follows cites the product the member sells as well as the means of selling, person to person or through a party plan.

For more information write or phone:

Direct Selling Association
1666 K St. NW, Ste. 1010,
Washington, DC 20006-2808;
(202) 293-5760.

Achievers Unlimited, Inc.
777 S. Flagler Dr., W. Tower, 9th Floor
West Palm Beach, FL 33401
(561) 835-3777
Person to person • nutrition products

Act II Jewelry, Inc.—Lady Remington
818 Thorndale Ave.
Bensenville, IL 60106
(800) 487-3323
Party plan • jewelry

AdvoCare International
11431-A Ferrell Ave.
Dallas, TX 75244
(214) 831-1033
Person to person • weight management and skin care products

Alliance U.S.A. Inc.
1100 E. Campbell
Richardson, TX 75081
(214) 783-4994
Person to person • nutrition products

AMC Corp.
595 Summer St.
Stanford, CT 06901
(203) 363-0331
Party plan • cookware, multicooking systems

American Coin Collectors, Inc.
3403 N. Pine Hills Rd.
Orlando, FL 32808
(407) 296-9457
Party plan and person to person • collectibles

American Communications Network, Inc.
100 W. Big Beaver Rd., Ste. 400
Troy, MI 48084
(810) 528-2500
Person to person • long-distance service,
debit calling cards, pay phones,
telecommunications services

Amway Corp.
7575 Fulton St. E
Ada, MI 49355-0001
(616) 787-6000
Person to person • home care and home
technology products, nutrition and personal care products, commercial products
and services

Applebrook Family Enrichment Network
PO Box 40
Fremont, MI 49412
(616) 924-7113
Party plan and person to person •
parenting and nutrition products

Art Finds International, Inc.
1810 S. Lynhurst Dr., Ste. A
Indianapolis, IN 46241
(317) 248-2666
Party plan • art

Artistic Impressions, Inc.
240 Cortland Ave.
Lombard, IL 60148
(630) 916-0050
Party plan • art

Assured Nutrition Plus
4279 Crumrine Rd.
Greenville, OH 45331
(513) 548-7713
Party plan and person to person • nutrition and weight management products

Avon Products, Inc.
9 W. 57th St.
New York, NY 10019
(800) FOR-AVON
Person to person • cosmetics, decorative
accessories, giftware, jewelry, skin care
and nutrition products, toys and games

Body Wise International, Inc.
6350 Palomar Oaks Ct.
Carlsbad, CA 92009
(619) 438-8977
Person to person • nutrition products

Book of Life
PO Box 6130
Grand Rapids, MI 49516
(800) 829-5233
Person to person • Bible-reading
program, educational materials

Brite International
3421 S. 500 W
PO Box 65688
Salt Lake City, UT 84115
(801) 263-9191
Party plan and person to person •
cassettes, books, videos, educational
materials

The Bron-Shoe Co.
1313 Alum Creek Dr.
Columbus, OH 43209
(614) 252-0967
Person to person • baby shoe bronzing

Busy Woman
9191 S. Main St.
Snowflake, AZ 85937
(520) 536-7705
Party plan • time management programs

Chambré International
PO Box 995
West Union, SC 29696
(864) 718-9119
Party plan and person to person • skin
care and nutrition products, home care
products, and cosmetics

Charmelle
101 Townsend St., Ste. 303
San Francisco, CA 94107
(415) 284-1684
Party plan and person to person •
jewelry

Cleveland Institute of Electronics, Inc.
1776 E. 17th St.
Cleveland, OH 44114
(216) 781-9400
Person to person • vocational training

Colesce Couture, Inc.
9004 Ambassador Row
Dallas, TX 75247
(214) 631-4860
Party plan • lingerie and sleepwear

Color Me Beautiful
14000 Thunderbolt Pl., Ste. E
Chantilly, VA 22021
(703) 471-6400
Party plan and person to person •
cosmetics, skin care products

Conklin Co., Inc.
551 Valley Park Dr.
PO Box 155
Shakopee, MN 55379
(612) 445-6010
Party plan and person to person •
personal care products, home care
products

Cookin' the American Way
11901 Grandview Rd.
Grandview, MO 64030
(800) 733-2465
Party plan • cookware

Cooks Know How
65 Mid County Dr.
Orchard Park, NY 14127
(716) 667-1543
Party plan • cookware

Country Neighbors, Inc.
304 E. 37th St.
Vancouver, WA 98663
(800) 681-8148
Party plan • crystal and china,
decorative accessories

The Country Peddlers & Company
of America, Inc.
5625 W. 5th St.
Alsip, IL 60482
(708) 597-1085
Party plan • decorative accessories

Creative Memories
2815 Clearwater Rd.
PO Box 767
St. Cloud, MN 56302
(800) 328-2344
Party plan • photo albums, photo
album supplies

CUTCO/Vector Corp.
1116 E. State St.
PO Box 1228
Olean, NY 14760-1228
(716) 372-3111
Person to person • cutlery

Designer Nutrition America
3535 Rte. 66, Bldg. 2
Neptune, NJ 07753
(908) 922-0777
Party plan and person to person • nutrition products, personal care products

Discovery Toys, Inc.
6400 Brisca St.
Livermore, CA 94550
(800) 426-4777
Party plan • toys and games, books, child-care products, educational materials, videos

DK Family Learning
7800 Southland Blvd., Ste. 200
Orlando, FL 32809
(407) 857-5463
Party plan and person to person • books, videos

Doncaster
Oak Springs Rd.
Box 1159
Rutherfordton, NC 28139
(800) 669-3662
Person to person • clothing, fashion accessories

DS-MAX U.S.A. Inc.
15 Chrysler St.
Irvine, CA 92718
(714) 587-9207
Person to person • books, business products, plants and foliage, toys and games, giftware, house- and kitchenwares

Dudley Products, Inc.
1080 Old Greensboro Rd.
Kernersville, NC 27284-3222
(910) 993-8800
Person to person • cosmetics, fragrances, skin and hair care products

Eagle Distributing Co., Inc.
7635 Main St.
PO Box 410
Fishees, NY 14453
(716) 924-2150
Person to person • fire alarms and extinguishers

Ekco Home Products Co.
2488 Townsgate Rd., Ste. A
Westlake Village, CA 91361
(805) 494-1711
Person to person • cookware, cutlery, water treatment systems

Electrolux Corp.
2300 Windy Ridge Pkwy., Ste. 900
Atlanta, GA 30339
(770) 933-1000
Person to person • vacuum cleaners, home care products

Encyclopedia Britannica, Inc.
Britannica Centre
310 S. Michigan Ave.
Chicago, IL 60604
(312) 347-7247
Person to person • encyclopedias, educational materials

Enrich International
748 N. 1340 W
Orem, UT 84057
(801) 226-2600
Party plan and person to person • health, fitness, and skin care products

ENVION International
472 Amherst St.
Nashua, NH 03063
(603) 881-7873
Person to person • nutrition and personal care products

Equinox International
1211 Town Center Dr.
Las Vegas, NV 89134
(702) 877-2257
Person to person • water treatment systems; air filters; nutrition products; cosmetics; hair, home, skin, and personal care products; and weight management products

Excel Communications, Inc.
8750 N. Central Expressway, Ste. 2000
Dallas, TX 75231
(214) 863-8000
Person to person • long-distance service

Finesse
668 Beale St.
Memphis, TN 38103-3205
(901) 526-1137
Party plan • jewelry

ForYou, Inc.
4235 Main St.
PO Box 1216
Loris, SC 29569
(803) 756-9000
Party plan and person to person • skin care products, self-improvement programs

The Fuller Brush Co.
One Fuller Way
PO Box 729
Great Bend, KS 67530
(800) 874-0016
Person to person • home and personal care products, house- and kitchenwares

Gold Marketing Associates
3403 N. Pine Hills Rd.
Orlando, FL 32808-2835
(407) 296-9457
Party plan and person to person • collectibles, jewelry

Golden Neo-Life Diamite International
3500 Gateway Blvd.
Fremont, CA 94537-5012
(510) 651-0405
Person to person • nutrition, home, and skin care products; water treatment systems; weight management products

Golden Pride/Rawleigh, Inc.
PO Box 21109
West Palm Beach, FL 33416-1109
(561) 640-5700
Person to person • nutrition products, weight management products, health and fitness products, house- and kitchenwares; water treatment systems; food and beverage products; skin care products

Goldilox USA, Inc.
6725 Millcreek Dr., Ste. 5
Mississauga, Ontario L5N SV3 Canada
(905) 567-9449
Person to person • cosmetics, skin, and
nutrition products

Herbalife International
PO Box 80210
Los Angeles, CA 90080-0210
(310) 410-960
Person to person • weight management,
nutrition, and personal care products;
fragrances

Highlights for Children, Inc.
2300 W. Fifth Ave.
PO Box 269
Columbus, OH 43216
(614) 486-0631
Person to person • educational materials

Home Interiors & Gifts, Inc.
4550 Spring Valley Rd.
Dallas, TX 75244-3705
(972) 386-1000
Party plan • decorative accessories,
giftware

The Homemakers Idea Co.
1420 Thorndale
Elk Grove Village, IL 60007
(800) 800-5452
Party plan • decorative accessories

House of Lloyd, Inc.
11901 Grandview Rd.
Grandview, MO 64030
(800) 733-2465
Party plan • Christmas decorations,
giftware, decorative accessories, toys
and games

H.Q. International, Inc.
1985  Forest La.
Garland, TX 75042
(972) 272-9400
Person to person • nutrition, skin, and
personal care products; auto care products

Hsin Ten Enterprise USA, Inc.
100 Commercial St.
Plainview, NY 11803
(516) 576-1616
Party plan and person
to person • health and fitness products

Hy Cite Corp.
333 Holtzman Rd.
Madison, WI 53713-2109
(608) 273-3373
Party plan and person to person •
cookware, crystal and china, water
treatment systems

Integrity International, Inc.
220 Reese Rd.
State College, PA 16801
(814) 237-9111
Person to person • stop-smoking, weight
management, and nutrition
products; long-distance service; fire alarms
and extinguishers

Intelligent Nutrients
321 Lincoln St., NE
Minneapolis, MN 55413
(612) 617-2000
Person to person • weight management
and nutrition products

Interior Design Nutritionals
75 W. Center St.
Provo, UT 84601
(801) 345-9000
Person to person • nutrition and weight
management products

Interstate Engineering
522 E. Vermont Ave.
Anaheim, CA 92805-5698
(714) 758-5011
Person to person • vacuum cleaners

Jafra Cosmetics International, Inc.
2451 Townsgate Rd.
Westlake Village, CA 91361
(800) 551-2345
Party plan and person to person • skin
care products, cosmetics, and fragrances

Jeunesse Cosmetics, Inc.
342 Madison Ave., Ste. 823
New York, NY 10173
(212) 682-7282
Party plan and person to person •
cosmetics, skin care products

Jeunique International, Inc.
19501 E. Walnut Dr.
PO Box 1950
City of Industry, CA 91749
(909) 598-8598
Party plan and person to person •
cosmetics, lingerie, and sleepwear;
nutrition and skin care products

JewelQuest
PO Box 749
Great Falls, VA 22066
(800) 771-4566
Party plan and person to person •
jewelry

KareMore International, Inc.
2401 S. 24th St.
Phoenix, AZ 85034
(602) 244-8976
Person to person • nutrition and weight
management products

Kids Only Clothing Club, Inc.
5775 Eleventh St. SE
Calgary, Alberta T2H 1M7 Canada
(403) 252-9667
Party plan • clothing

The Kirby Co.
1920 W. 114 St.
Cleveland, OH 44102-2391
(216) 228-2400
Person to person • vacuum cleaners

Kitchen Fair
1090 Redmond Rd.
PO Box 100
Jacksonville, AR 72076
Party plan • cookware, decorative
accessories, house- and kitchenwares

Kizure Products Co., Inc.
1950 N. Central Ave.
Compton, CA 90222
(310) 604-0032
Person to person • hair care products

Lady Love Skin Care
PO Box 7687
Plano, TX 75086-7687
(214) 596-5239
Party Plan and person to person •
skin care products

Lanclé, Inc.
800 Third Ave., 36th Fl.
New York, NY 10022
(212) 308-3383
Party plan and person to person •
cosmetics; skin, hair, and personal care
products; fashion accessories

LifeRich Limited Co.
360 B St.
PO Box 51980
Idaho Falls, ID 83405-1980
(208) 525-7850
Person to person • nutrition and personal
care products

The Longaberger Co.
95 Chestnut St.
Dresden, OH 43821-9600
(800) 966-0374
Party Plan • decorative
accessories, house- and kitchenwares

Longevity Network, Ltd.
15 Cactus Garden Dr.
Henderson, NV 89014
(702) 454-7000
Person to person • nutrition, skin, hair,
and personal care products

Market America, Inc.
7605-A Business Park Dr.
Greensboro, NC 27409
(910) 605-0040
Person to person • personal, home,
and auto care products; photography;
nutrition products

Mary Kay, Inc.
16251 Dallas Pkwy.
Dallas, TX 75248
(800) MARY-KAY
Party plan and person to person •
cosmetics, skin care products

Masterguard Corp.
155 Howell St.
Dallas, TX 75207
(214) 651-7300
Party plan and person to person •
fire alarms and extinguishers

Melaleuca, Inc.
3910 S. Yellowstone Hwy.
Idaho Falls, ID 83402
(208) 522-0700
Person to person • nutrition products,
personal and home care products

Melissa Rice and Co.
6937 Flintlock
Houston, TX 77040
(800) 345-1133
Party plan and person to person •
clothing, home accessories

Multiples At Home
1431 Regal Row
Dallas, TX 75247
(800) 727-8875
Party plan • clothing

Muscle Dynamics Fitness Network, Inc.
20100 Hamilton Ave.
Torrance, CA 90502
(310) 715-8036
Person to person • health and fitness,
nutrition, and weight management
products

National Telephone &
Communications, Inc.
2801 Main St.
Irvine, CA 92614
(714) 251-8000
Person to person • long-distance service

Natural World
7373 N. Scottsdale Rd., Ste. A-280
Scottsdale, AZ 85253
(602) 905-1110
Person to person • skin, hair, and home
care products; nutrition products

Nature's Sunshine Products, Inc.
75 E. 1700 S
PO Box 19005
Provo, UT 84605-9005
(801) 342-4300
Person to person • nutrition and skin
care products, water treatment systems,
cookware

Nest Entertainment, Inc.
6100 Colwell Blvd.
Irving, TX 75039
(214) 402-7100
Party plan and person to person • Bible
videotapes, audiotapes, educational
materials

New Image International, Inc.
PO Box 1038
Georgetown, KY 40324
(502) 867-1895
Person to person • weight management
and nutrition products

Newone Cosmetics Corp.
4525 Wilshire Blvd., Ste. 140
Los Angeles, CA 90010
(213) 930-1701
Party plan and person to person •
cosmetics; skin care and nutrition
products

Nikken, Inc.
15363 Barranca Pkwy.
Irvine, CA 92618
(714) 789-2000
Party plan and person to person •
bedding, nutrition products

Noevir USA, Inc.
1095 SE Main St.
Irvine, CA 92714
(800) USA-8888
Person to person • cosmetics, skin care
and nutrition products

NSA
4260 E. Raines Rd.
Memphis, TN 38118
(901) 366-9288
Person to person • air filters, water treatment systems, educational materials,
nutrition products

Nu Skin International, Inc.
75 W. Center St.
Provo, UT 84601
(801) 345-1000
Party plan and person to person •
cosmetics, nutrition products, skin and
home care products

Nutrix International, LLC
2001 N. Clybourn Ave., Ste. 403
Chicago, IL 60614
(800) 468-8749
Party plan and person to person • health care apparel

Oriflame U.S.A.
4630 Cerritos Ave.
Los Alamitos, CA 90720
(800) 959-0699
Person to person • skin care and nutrition products, cosmetics, fragrances

Oxyfresh Worldwide, Inc.
E. 12928 Indiana Ave.
PO Box 3723
Spokane, WA 99220
(509) 924-4999
Person to person • dental hygiene products; animal care products and food; nutrition products; skin, personal, hair, and home care products

Oxygen for Life, Inc.
1290 San Marcos Blvd.
San Marcos, CA 92069
(800) 619-6994
Person to person • stabilized oxygen, weight management products, nutrition products

The Pampered Chef, Ltd.
350 S. Rohlwing Rd.
Addison, IL 60101-3079
(708) 261-8900
Party plan • house- and kitchenwares

PartyLife Gifts, Inc.
PO Box 976
Plymouth, MA 02362-0976
(508) 830-3100
Party plan • candles, candle accessories

Personal Creations Gift Shows, Inc.
530 Executive Dr.
Willowbrook, IL 60521
(630) 655-3200
Party plan • personalized gifts

Petra Fashions, Inc.
35 Cherry Hill Pk.
Danvers, MA 01923
(508) 777-5853
Party plan • lingerie and sleepwear

Pfaltzgraff/Flemington Outlet Corp.
140 E. Market St.
York, PA 17401
(717) 848-5500
Party plan and person to person • tableware

Pola U.S.A., Inc.
251 E. Victoria St.
Carson, CA 90746
(310) 527-9696
Party plan and person to person • skin and hair care products, cosmetics, fragrances

Premier Designs, Inc.
1551 Corporate Dr.
Irving, TX 85038-2431
(800) 486-SERV
Party plan and person to person • jewelry

Primerica Financial Services
3120 Breckenridge Blvd.
Duluth, GA 30199-0001
(770) 381-1000
Person to person • financial and investment services, insurance

Princess House, Inc.
455 Somerset Ave.
North Dighton, MA 02754
(800) 622-0039
Party plan • decorative accessories, crystal and china, jewelry

PRP Wine International, Inc.
1701 Howard St.
Elk Grove Village, IL 60007
(847) 290-7800
Person to person • wine

RACHAeL International
1706 E. Semoran Blvd., Ste. 114
Apopka, FL 32703
(800) 366-3806
Party plan and person to person • skin and hair care products, cosmetics, nutrition products

Regal Ware, Inc.
1675 Reigle Dr.
Kewaskum, WI 53040
(414) 626-2121
Party plan and person to person • cookware, cutlery, tableware, water treatment systems

Reliv, Inc.
PO Box 405
Chesterfield, MO 63006-0405
(314) 537-9715
Person to person • nutrition and personal care products

Rena-Ware Distributors, Inc.
PO Box 97050
Redmond, WA 98073-9750
(206) 881-6171
Party plan and person to person • cookware

Rexair, Inc.
3221 W. Big Beaver Rd., Ste. 200
Troy, MI 48084
(810) 643-7222
Person to person • vacuum cleaners, home care products

Rexall Showcase International
853 Broken Sound Pkwy NW
Boca Raton, FL 33487-3694
(561) 994-2090
Person to person • health and fitness products, nutrition products, water treatment systems, personal care products

Rich Plan Corp.
4981 Commercial Dr.
Yorkville, NY 13495
(800) 243-1358
Person to person • food and beverage products, home appliances

RMC Group, Inc.
2969 Interstate St.
Charlottte, NC 28208
(704) 393-1860
Party plan and person to person • skin care and nutrition products, fragrances, cosmetics

Saladmaster, Inc.
912 113th St.
Arlington, TX 76011-5407
(817) 633-3555
Party plan and person to person •
cookware, tableware

Seaborne, Inc.
6200 Windward Pkwy.
Alpharetta, GA 30202
(770) 663-633
Party plan and person to person •
nutrition products

Shaklee Corp.
Shaklee Terr., 444 Market St.
San Francisco, CA 94111
(415) 954-3000
Person to person • nutrition products,
personal and home care products, water
treatment systems

Shaperite
9850 S. 300 W
Sandy, UT 84070
(801) 562-3600
Person to person • weight management
and personal care products

Society Corp.
1515 W. Kilgore Ave.
Muncie, IN 47304
(317) 289-3318
Person to person • cookware, crystal
and china, cutlery, tableware, water
treatment systems

The Southwestern Co.
PO Box 305140
Nashville, TN 37230-5140
(615) 391-2500
Person to person • books, educational
material

Sportron International, Inc.
1249 Commerce
Richardson, TX 75081
(800) 843-1202
Person to person • nutritional and weight
management products, skin and home
care products

Stanley Home Products
50 Payson Ave.
East Hampton, MA 01027
(413) 527-4001
Party plan and person to person • home
and personal care products

Stef International Corp.
6870 Goreway Dr.
Mississauga, Ontario L4V IP1, Canada
(905) 672-3212
Person to person • personal care and
nutrition products

The Story Teller
208 E. 800 S, PO Box 921
Salem, UT 84653
(801) 423-2560
Party plan • books, educational materials,
cassettes, toys and games

Success Motivation Institute
1600 Lake Air Dr.
Waco, TX 76710
(817) 776-1230
Person to person • self-improvement and
time management programs

Sunrider International
1625 Abalone Ave.
Torrance, CA 90501
(310) 781-3808
Party plan and person to person •
nutrition products; home, skin, and
personal care products; cosmetics

Symmetry Corp.
420 S. Hillview Dr.
Milpitas, CA 95035
(408) 942-7700
Party plan and person to person •
nutrition and weight management
products

Table Charm Corp.
248 Steelcase Rd. E
Markham, Ontario L3R IG2, Canada
(905) 470-7861
Person to person • cookware, tableware

Tiara Exclusives
717 E St.
Dunkirk, IN 47336
(317) 768-7821
Party plan • decorative accessories,
tableware

Totally Tropical Interiors, Ltd.
4310 Twelfth St. NE, Ste. 100
Calgary, Alberta T2E 6K9, Canada
(403) 291-9366
Party plan • plants, foliage, decorative
accessories

Tri-Chem, Inc.
One Cape May St.
Harrison, NJ 07029
(201) 482-5500
Party plan • crafts

Tupperware Corp.
PO Box 2353
Orlando, FL 32802-2353
(407) 826-5050
Party plan and person to person • house-
and kitchenwares, toys and games

United Consumers Club, Inc.
8450 S. Broadway
Merrillville, IN 46410
(219) 736-1100
Party plan • group buying service

U.S. Safety & Engineering Corp.
2365 El Camino Ave.
Sacramento, CA 95821
(916) 482-8888
Person to person • security systems
and devices

USANA, Inc.
3838 W. Parkway Blvd.
West Valley City, UT 84120
(801) 954-7200
Party plan and person to person •
nutrition and skin care products

Usborne Books at Home
10302 E. 55 Pl.
Tulsa, OK 74146
(800) 475-4522
Party plan and person to person • books

Vita Craft Corp.
11100 W. 58th St.
PO Box 3129
Shawnee, KS 66203
(913) 631-6265
Party plan and person to person •
cookware, crystal and china, cutlery,
tableware, water treatment systems

Viva America Marketing, Inc.
1239 Victoria St.
Costa Mesa, CA 92627
(800) 243-8482
Party plan and person to person •
nutrition, skin care, weight management
and fitness products

Watkins Inc.
150 Liberty St.
Winona, MN 55987-0570
(507) 457-3300
Party plan and person to person •
food and beverage products, health and
fitness products

Weekender Casual Wear, Inc.
1485 Busch Pkwy.
Buffalo Grove, IL 60089
(847) 465-1666
Party plan • clothing

The West Bend Co.
400 Washington St.
West Bend, WI 53095
(414) 334-6935
Party plan and person to person •
cookware, water treatment systems

Wicker Plus, Ltd.
N112 W. 14600 Mequon Rd.
Germantown, WI 53022
(414) 255-7377
Party plan • decorative accessories

The Workshops of Gerald E. Henn
1001 Country Way
Warren, OH 44481
(330) 824-2575
Party plan • decorative accessories

World Book, Inc.
525 W. Monroe St., 20th Fl.
Chicago, IL 60661
(312) 258-3933
Person to person • encyclopedias,
educational materials

Youngevity, Inc.
4951 Airport Pkwy.—500
Dallas, TX 75248
(800) 469-6864
Person to person • nutrition products

# Franchises Suitable for Home Business

The list that follows was compiled by the Minority Business Development Agency of the U.S. Department of Commerce.

A-Pro Services
PO Box 132
Harding Hwy.
Newfield, NJ 08344
(800) 467-2776, (609) 697-1000
Equity capital needed: $6,000–$7,000
($10,700 total start-up)
Franchise fee: $7,000
Royalty fee: $200 per month
Comprises carpet and upholstery dyeing and cleaning, tinting, fiber protection, carpet repair, flood and water-damage restoration, odor control, floor covering installation, and shop-at-home floor covering sales.

Aloette Cosmetics
1301 Wright's La. E
West Chester, PA 19380
(800) 321-2563, (215) 692-0600
Equity capital needed: $35,000–$65,000
Franchise fee: $10,000–$20,000
Royalty fee: 5%
Provides aloe-vera skin care products, as well as cosmetics. Products marketed primarily through home shows.

Bride's Day
750 Hamburg Turnpike, #208
Pompton Lakes, NJ 07442
(201) 835-6551
Equity capital needed: $5,000–$10,000
Franchise fee: $14,900
Royalty fee: 6%
A free community magazine dedicated to assisting the bride with all aspects of wedding planning, while offering an affordable advertising vehicle to local wedding-related businesses.

Canine Counselors
1660 Southern Blvd.
West Palm Beach, FL 33406
(800) 456-DOGS, (407) 640-3970
Equity capital needed: $39,000
Franchise fee: $29,000
Royalty fee: 7% or $100 per week minimum.
Professional dog training and behavior problem solving. Schools provide services in client's home or business, with lifetime training warranty.

Carpet Network
109 Gaither Dr., #302
Mt. Laurel, NJ 08054
(800) 428-1067, (609) 273-9393
Equity capital needed: $2,000–$4,000
Franchise fee: $13,500
Royalty fee: 5% on gross sales
Mobile carpet and window treatment
business.

The Cat's Pajamas
PO Box 48
Lincolnville, ME 04849
(207) 789-5139
Equity capital needed: $30,000–$40,000
Franchise fee: $10,000
Royalty fee: 5% of annual gross revenues
Boarding and grooming facility that caters
to felines and their owners.

Complete Music
7877 L St.
Omaha, NE 68127
(800) 843-3866, (402) 339-0001
Equity capital needed: $15,000–$20,000
Franchise fee: $9,500 for major market
Royalty fee: 8%
Provides entertainment for special events.

Computertots
10132 Colvin Run Rd.
Great Falls, VA 22063
(800) 531-5053
Equity capital needed: $24,000–$40,000
Franchise fee: $15,900–$23,900
Royalty Fee: 6% or $250
Offers early-childhood computer educa-
tion through day-care centers, preschools,
and community centers.

Direct Opinions
23600 Mercantile Rd.
Beachwood, OH 44122
(216) 831-7979
Equity capital needed: $22,150–$51,800
Franchise fee: $10,000–$25,000
Royalty fee: 6% of first $100,000, 4%
thereafter
Specializes in customer-satisfaction surveys for retail sales and service clients,
market research surveys, and lead genera-
tion services. Home-based telemarketers
conduct the phone calls. Reporting and
recordkeeping are accomplished through
the use of proprietary computer software
programs.

Dr. Vinyl & Associates
13665 E. 42nd Terr. S, #H
Independence, MO 64055
(800) 531-6600, (816) 478-0800
Equity capital needed: $19,500
Franchise fee: $19,500
Royalty fee: 4–7%
Provides mobile repair, reconditioning,
and aftermarket sales and services to auto
dealers and other commercial accounts.

Drapery Works Systems
4640 Western Ave.
Lisle, IL 60532
(800) 353-7273, (708) 963-2820
Equity capital needed: $5,000
Franchise fee: $7,500
Royalty fee: 5%
Custom drapery and bedding accessories
business.

Emerald Green Lawn Care
9333 N. Meridian St.
Indianapolis, IN 46260
(800) 783-0981, (317) 846-9940
Equity capital needed: $60,000–$90,000
Franchise fee: $15,000
Royalty fee: 8.5–6.5%
Full-service residential lawn, tree, and shrub care.

The Fourth R
1715 Market St., #103
Kirkland, WA 98033
(800) 821-8653, (206) 828-0336
Equity capital needed: $17,000–$20,000
Franchise fee: $16,000 first franchise, $7,500 each additional (initial franchise fee includes two computers and software.)
Royalty fee: 5–9%
Franchisees teach computer skills to children 3 to 14 years old. Broad curriculum includes ESL program and introductory classes for adults.

Furniture Medic
277 Southfield Pkwy., #130
Forest Park, GA 30050
(800) 877-9933, (404) 361-9933
Equity capital needed: $5,600–$10,000
Franchise fee: $7,000
Royalty fee: $200 per month
Furniture Medic is an on-site furniture restoration and repair franchise.

Haunted Hayrides
135 Old Cove Rd., Ste. 210
Liverpool, NY 13090
(800) 344-2868, (315) 453-6009
Equity capital needed: $30,000–$45,000
Franchise fee: $15,000

Royalty fee: 10% ($5,000 minimum)
Hayrides during the month of October, with a Halloween theme. Acts and actors are positioned on a trail or road.

House of Blinds & More
2300 W. Eight Mile Rd.
Southfield, MI 48034
(313) 357-4710
Equity capital needed: $26,000–$86,500 (mobile van), $54,000–$117,000 (retail store)
Franchise fee: $15,000
Royalty fee: 5%
Sells and installs window treatments and related products and services.

Kitchen Tune-Up
131 N. Roosevelt
Aberdeen, SD 57401
(800) 333-6385, (605) 225-4049
Equity capital needed: $15,000–$25,000
Franchise fee: $11,500
Royalty fee: 7%
Provides inexpensive wood care to home-owners and owners of commercial property. Also offers door replacement materials.

Lifestyle Mobile Carpet Showroom
PO Box 3876
Dallas, GA 30721
(800) 346-4531, (706) 673-6252
Equity capital needed: $9,000–$12,000
Franchise fee: $9,999
Royalty fee: 5%
Mobile showroom sells carpet directly to the homeowner in his or her home.

Magis Fund Raising Specialists
845 Heathermoor La., #961
Perrysburg, OH 43551
(419) 244-6711
Equity capital needed: $28,500–$52,500
Franchise fee: $7,500
Royalty fee: 8% or $200 per month
minimum
Provides full-service fund-raising, financial,
development, marketing, and public relations services to nonprofit organizations.

Mr. Trees
PO Box 1609
San Anselmo, CA 94960
(415) 485-1180
Equity capital needed: $100,000
Franchise fee: $28,500
Royalty fee: 6%
Provides environmentally sound tree and
shrub care.

National Property Registry
PO Box 72376
Marietta, GA 30007
(800) 971-5201, (404) 971-5200
Equity capital needed: Less than $25,000
Franchise fee: $19,950
Royalty fee: $500 per year association fee
A nationwide video inventory system
for businesses and homeowners offers
security and documentation.

Petential
22201 DuPont, #400
Irvine, CA 92715
(714) 675-9546
Equity capital needed: $25,000–$38,000
Franchise fee: $12,500
Royalty fee: 6%
Home-delivery of pet food and pet care
products.

Pet Nanny of America
1000 Long Blvd., #9
Lansing, MI 48911
(517) 694-4400
Equity capital needed: $1,500–$4,500
Franchise fee: $8,700
Royalty fee: 5% or $25 per week
minimum
Provides in-home pet care and services for
absent homeowners.

Pets Are Inn
7723 Tanglewood Ct., #150
Minneapolis, MN 55439
(800) 248-PETS, (612) 944-8298
Equity capital needed: $25,000–$35,000
Franchise fee: $12,000
Royalty fee: 10% or monthly minimums
Boards pets in private homes.

Profusion Systems
2851 S. Parker Rd., #650
Aurora, CO 80014
(800) 777-3873, (303) 337-1949
Equity capital needed: $15,000–$30,000
Franchise fee: $20,500
Royalty fee: 6%
Plastic, vinyl, leather, and laminate
repair for restaurants, hotels, airports,
hospitals, etc.

Shoecrafters
2310 W. Bell Rd., #8
Phoenix, AZ 85023
(602) 863-6985
Equity capital needed: $9,000–$10,000
Franchise fee: $4,995
Royalty fee: $100 per month
Mobile shoe retail and service franchise in
a service route format, calling on profes-
sionals in their workplace.

The Sports Section
3120 Medlock Bridge Rd., Bldg. A
Norcross, GA 30071
(800) 321-9127, (404) 416-6604
Equity capital needed: $14,900–$31,500
Franchise fee: $14,900–$31,500
Royalty fee: 0%
A home-based franchise in youth sports
photography, offering over 100 keepsakes
with a child's individual and team picture.

Terra Systems
PO Box 220706
Charlotte, NC 28222
(704) 522-0310
Equity capital needed: $35,000
Franchise fee: $22,000
Royalty fee: 7%
Organic and organic-based lawn care ser-
vices, integrated pest management–based
tree and shrub care.

Two Men and a Truck/USA
1915 E. Michigan Ave.
Lansing, MI 48912
(800) 345-1070, (517) 482-MOVE
Equity capital needed: $25,000–$35,000
Franchise fee: $17,950
Royalty fee: 4%
Local moving-company franchise. Sells
boxing and packing supplies.

Video Data Services
30 Grove St.
Pittsford, NY 14534
(800) 836-9461, (716) 385-4773
Equity capital needed: $20,000
Franchise fee: $17,950
Royalty fee: $500 annually

Video, photography, film-to-tape trans-
fers, video editing, and special effects.

Wee Watch Private Home Day Care
105 Main St.
Unionville, ON L3R 2G1 Canada
(905) 479-4274
Equity capital needed: $15,000
Franchise fee: $6,000
Royalty fee: 8%
A private home day-care agency, where a
franchisee recruits, trains, and supervises
women to do day care in their own
homes. Parents needing care contact the
agency for placement. A full day-care
program is in place.

Window-Ology
770-B N. Main St.
Orange, CA 92668
(800) 303-2300, (714) 997-9675
Equity capital needed: $3,000–$5,000
Franchise fee: $20,000
Royalty fee: 5%
Sales and installation of window cover-
ings. Offers shopping at home.

Yard Cards
2940 W. Main St.
Belleville, IL 62223
(618) 233-0491
Equity capital needed: $5,000–$15,000
Franchise fee: $1,000 minimum
Royalty fee: 5%
Rents 8-foot greeting cards for all
occasions.

# Institutions Accredited by the Distance Education and Training Council

For more than 70 years, the Distance Education and training Council (DETC, formerly the National Home Study Council) has been the standard-setting agency for distance-education institutions. Its accrediting program employs procedures similar to those of other nationally recognized education-accrediting associations.

According to the council, each accredited school

- Has a competent faculty
- Offers educationally sound and up-to-date courses
- Carefully screens students for admission
- Provide satisfactory educational services
- Has demonstrated ample student success and satisfaction
- Advertises its courses truthfully
- Is financially able to deliver high-quality educational service

For information about any institution listed in this appendix, write directly to the institution. For information about distance education or the DETC accrediting program, write to Michael P. Lambert, Executive Secretary, Accrediting Commission, Distance Education and Training Council, 1601 18th St. NW, Washington, DC 20009-2529.

The dates shown in parentheses after the date founded indicate when the school was first accredited and the year of the next scheduled reaccreditation review.

American Academy of Nutrition
Sequoyah Hills Center
1200 Kenesaw
Knoxville, TN 37919-7736
(800) 290-4226
Fax: (423) 524-1692

e-mail: aantn@aol.com
Internet: http://www.hithmall.com
Founded 1985 (1989/2000). Individual courses, diploma program in comprehensive nutrition, Associate of Science degree in applied nutrition.

American College of Prehospital
Medicine
365 Canal St., Ste. 2300
New Orleans, LA 70130
(503) 561-6543
Fax: (504) 561-6585
Internet: http://www.acpm.edu
Founded 1991 (1994/99). Associate of
Science degrees in emergency medical ser-
vices and hazardous materials technology,
and Bachelor of Science in emergency
medical services.

American Health Information
Management Association
919 N. Michigan Ave., Ste. 1400
Chicago, IL 60611-1683
(312) 787-2672
Fax: (312) 787-9793
e-mail: info@ahima.mhs.compuserve.com
Founded 1928 (1970/2000). Courses in
medical record technology and coding.

American Military University
9104-P Manassas Dr.
Manassas Park, VA 20111
(703) 330-5398
Fax: (703) 330-5109
e-mail: amugen@amunet.edu
Internet: http://www.amunet.edu
Founded 1991 (1995/99). Master of arts
in military studies, bachelor of arts in military history, military management, and
intelligence studies.

American School
2200 E. 170th St.
Lansing, IL 60438
(708) 418-2800
Founded 1897 (1956/97). Complete high
school diploma program.

Army Institute for Professional
Development
U.S. Army Training Support Center
Ft. Eustis, VA 23604-5121
e-mail: mottern@eustis-emh1.army.mil,
Internet: http://www.atscarmy.org
Founded 1976 (1978/99). U.S. Army
specialist and professional development
courses. Enrollment is restricted to active
and reserve component military personnel, federal civil service personnel, ROTC
cadets, and allied military students.

Art Instruction Schools
3309 Broadway NE
(612) 339-6656
Fax: (612) 362-5260
Minneapolis, MN 55413
Founded 1914 (1956/2000). Courses in
art and fiction and nonfiction writing.

Atlantic University
Atlantic Ave. at 67th St.
PO Box 595
Virginia Beach, VA 23451-0595
(800) 428-1512
Founded 1930 (1994/99). Master of arts
in transpersonal studies.

Berean University
1445 Boonville Ave.
Springfield, MO 65802
(800) 443-1083
Fax: (417) 862-5218
e-mail: Berean@ag.org
Internet: http://www.berean.edu
Founded 1948 (1985/2000). A division of
the Assemblies of God. Graduate
degrees and nondegree courses in Bible
studies, evangelism, and theological areas.

The Boyd School, Travel Lab Division
1412 Beers School Rd.
Moon Township, PA 15108
(800) 245-6673
Fax: (412) 299-2222
e-mail: BoydSchool@aol.com
Founded 1968 (1979/99). Airline and
travel education program with optional
four-week resident program.

Breastfeeding Support Consultants
Center for Lactation Education
228 Park La.
Chalfont, PA 18914
(215) 822-1281
Founded 1981 (1995/2000). A division of
Breastfeeding Support Consultants. Lactation consultation and breastfeeding counselor courses with optional combination
distance study–resident training.

California College for Health Sciences
222 W. 24th St.
National City, CA 91950
(619) 477-4800
Fax: (619) 477-4360
e-mail: cchsinfo@cchs.edu
Internet: http://www.cchs.edu
Founded 1976 (1981/96). A subsidiary of
ICS Learning Systems. Associate degrees
in respiratory care, medical transcription,
electroencephalographic technology,
allied health, and early childhood education. A bachelor of science in health
services with emphases in management,
polysomnography, and respiratory
therapy. A master of science in community health administration and wellness
promotion.

Cambridge Academy
1111 S.W. 17th St.
Ocala, FL 34474
(800) 252-3777
Founded 1978 (1990/99). Comprehensive
instruction for grades 6–12, meets
180-day requirements. Also offers
college preparation, remedial, and adult
education programs. Graduates earn high
school diploma.

The Catholic Distance University
39959 Catoctin Ridge St.
PO Box 178
Paeonian Springs, VA 20129-0178
(888) 254-4CDU
e-mail: cdu@ewtn.com
Founded 1983 (1986/2000). Catachetical
diploma and college credit options.
Courses in Catholic doctrine, moral
theology, sacraments, scripture, history,
spirituality, medical ethics, mariology,
catechetics, and the laity.

Citizens' High School
188 College Dr.
Orange Park, FL 32067
(904) 276-1700
Founded 1981 (1984/97). Complete high
school diploma program.

Cleveland Institute of Electronics, Inc.
1776 E. 17th St.
Cleveland, OH 44114
(800) 243-6446
Founded 1934 (1956/97). Degree and
nondegree courses in electronics engineering, electronics technology, broadcast
engineering, color-TV troubleshooting,
electronic communications, and digital
and microprocessor technology.

College for Financial Planning
4695 S. Monaco St.
Denver, CO 80237-3403
(303) 220-1200
Founded 1972 (1995/2000). Master of science degree with an emphasis in financial planning.

Diamond Council of America
9140 Ward Pkwy.
Kansas City, MO 64114
Founded 1944 (1984/98). Courses in diamontology and gemology leading to certificates for diamontologists and guild gemologists. Courses offered to members of the Diamond Council of America and their employees.

Educational Institute of the American Hotel & Motel Association
Stephen S. Nisbet Bldg.
1407 S. Harrison Rd.
PO Box 1240
East Lansing, MI 48826
(800) 344-3320
Fax: (517) 353-5527
Internet: http://www.eiahma.org
Founded 1951 (1963/98). Courses and certification programs in hotel–motel, restaurant, and food service operations.

Emergency Management Institute, Federal Emergency Management Agency
16825 S. Seton Ave.
Emmitsburg, MD 21727
Founded 1967 (1988/97). Federally sponsored courses in emergency preparedness.

The English Language Institute of America, Inc.
(717) 941-3406
925 Oak St., Scranton, PA 18515
Founded 1942 (1981/99). Courses entitled Practical English and the Command of Words and Real-Life Math.

Extension Course Institute
United States Air Force
50 S. Turner Blvd.
Maxwell AFB
Gunter Annex, AL 36118-5643
(334) 416-4252
Founded 1950 (1975/2000). U.S. Air Force professional military education, career development, and specialized technical courses. Enrollment is restricted to active-duty military, Air Force Reserve, Air National Guard, civil service, and other specified personnel.

Gemological Institute of America
1660 Stewart St.
Santa Monica, CA 90404-4088
(310) 829-2991
Founded 1931 (1965/96). Courses in diamonds, diamond grading, colored stones, gem identification, color stone grading, pearls, pearl and bead stringing, jewelry display, fine jewelry sales, counter sketching, advanced find jewelry sales, and gold and precious metals.

Grantham College of Engineering
34641 Grantham College Rd.
PO Box 5700
Slidell, LA 70469-5700
(504) 649-4191
e-mail: gogce@aol.com *or*
76771.1630@compuserve.com
Founded 1951 (1961/2000). Associate
and bachelor degrees in electronics engineering technology, computer engineering
technology, and computer science.

Griggs University
12501 Old Columbia Pike
PO Box 4437
Silver Spring, MD 20914-4437
(301) 680-6570
Founded 1990. Associate of arts degree
in personal ministries, bachelor of arts
degree in religion, bachelor of arts degree
in theological studies, adult education,
and independent study. (Send inquiries
to box number.)

The Hadley School for the Blind
700 Elm St.
Winnetka, IL 60093
(800) 323-4238
Founded 1920 (1958/99). Over 100
courses offered. High school, independent
living, recreational, and technical subjects.
Taught by Braille or audiocassettes. Also
offers courses for sighted families of blind
children and adults. No tuition charged.

Hemphill Schools
2562 E. Colorado Blvd.
Pasadena, CA 91107-3744
(818) 568-8148
Fax: (818) 568-4994

Founded 1920 (1966/96). Spanish-
language courses in patternmaking and
dressmaking, computer networks, radio-
TV repair, electricity, air conditioning,
video repair, refrigeration, English (ESL),
automotive electronics/electricity, automotive mechanics, and computer maintenance and repair.

Home Study International
12501 Old Columbia Pike
PO Box 4437
Silver Spring, MD 29014-4437
(301) 680-6570
Founded 1909 (1967/98). Correspondence courses for preschool, kindergarten,
elementary (grades 1–6), junior high,
secondary (with diploma), and college
students. Adult education and independent study also available. (Send inquiries
to box number.)

Hospitality Training Center
220 N. Main St.
Hudson, OH 44236
(216) 653-9151
Founded 1961 (1986/96). Course in motel
management training.

Hypnosis Motivation Institute
Extension School
18607 Ventura Blvd., Ste. 310
Tarzana, CA 91356
(800) 6000-HMI
Founded 1967 (1989/98). Professional
training in hypnosis and hypnotherapy.

ICI University
6300 N. Belt Line Rd.
Irving, TX 75063
(800) 444-0424
e-mail: info@ici.edu
Internet: http://www.ici.edu
An institution of the Division of Foreign
Missions of the Assemblies of God, Springfield, MO. Founded 1967 (1977/98).
Degree and nondegree courses in Bible
studies, evangelism, and theological areas.

ICS Center for Degree Studies
925 Oak St.
Scranton, PA 18515
(717) 342-7701
Founded 1974. Specialized associate
degree in business, computer science,
engineering technology, electronics
technology, and hospitality.

ICS Learning Systems
(same phone and address as above.)
Founded 1890 (1956/99). Courses at the
secondary and postsecondary levels in
technology, engineering, business, vocational trades, practical arts, and specialized
industrial subjects.

ICS-Newport/Pacific High School
(same phone and address as above.)
Founded 1972. Complete high school
diploma program.

IMC-International Management Centres
Castle St.
Buckingham, England MK18 1BP
44-1280-817222
Founded 1964 (1989/99). Courses and
degree programs in general management
and all major fields of professional
management.

Institute of Physical Therapy
170 Malaga St.
St. Augustine, FL 32084
(904) 826-0084
Founded 1979 (1993/98). Combination
distance study and resident courses
leading to a postprofessional master of science in physical therapy.

International Aviation and
Travel Academy
300 W. Arbrook Blvd.
Arlington, TX 76014-3199
(800) 678-0700
Founded 1971 (1988/97). Distance study
and combination distance study-resident
courses in airline and travel industry
fields.

International School of
Information Management
501 S. Cherry St., Ste. 350
Denver, CO 80222
(800) 441-ISIM
Fax: (303) 336-1144
Founded 1987 (1993/98). Master of
science in information management and
master of business administration.

John Tracy Clinic
806 W. Adams Blvd.
Los Angeles, CA 90007
(800) 522-4582
Founded 1942 (1965/97). Courses for
parents of preschool deaf children and
deaf-blind children. No tuition charged.

Keystone National High School
420 W. 5th St.
PO Box 616
Bloomsburg, PA 17815
(717) 784-5220
e-mail: kschool@mail.prolog.net
Internet: http://keystone.ptd.net
Founded 1995. A complete high school
diploma program with both college and
career preparation options.

Learning and Evaluation Center
(same phone and address as above.)
Founded 1972 (1985/99). "Summer
school" offering extensions in general subject areas to 5th- through 12th-grade
students who fail during their regular
school year. Student's school approval required. English and math skill reinforce-
ment programs for all grades and adults.

Lifetime Career Schools
(717) 876-6340
101 Harrison St.
Archbald, PA 18403
Founded 1944 (1957/2000). Diploma programs in landscaping, flower arranging
and floristry, sewing and dressmaking,
doll repair, secretarial and bookkeeping
skills, cooking, and small-business
management.

Marine Corps Institute
Marine Barracks, 8th and I Sts. SE
Washington, DC 20390-5000
(202) 433-2728
Founded 1920 (1977/97). Courses, programs, and materials designed to improve
the occupational skills and professional
military education of marines. Enrollment
is restricted to active-duty military person-

nel, retired marines, reserve marines,
civilian employees of the Department of
Defense, and allied military students.

Microcomputer Technology Center
14904 Jefferson Davis Hwy., Ste. 411
Woodbridge, VA 22191
(800) 448-2077
e-mail: 100315.3442.compuserve.com
Founded 1989 (1992/96). Courses in
computer operations.

Modern Gun School
500 N. Kimball Ave., Ste. 105
Southlake, TX 76092
(800) 774-5112
Fax: (800) 556-5112
Founded 1946 (1970/2001). A division of
Distance Learning International. Courses
in basic and advanced gun repair and
gunsmithing.

National Association Medical
Staff Services
9724 Kingston Pike, Ste. 701
Knoxville, TN 37922
(423) 531-7074
Fax: (423) 531-9939
Founded 1978 (1996/2000). Courses
in medical office administration, medical
terminology, overview of medical
staff organization, overview of health-
care accreditation, and basic elements of
medical staff law.

National College of Appraisal and Property
Management
3597 Parkway La., Ste. 100
Norcross, GA 30092
(800) 362-7070
Founded 1987 (1993/97). Courses in
real-estate appraisal and property
management.

National Distance Education Center
500 N. Kimball Ave., Ste. 105
Southlake, TX 76092
(800) 664-5112
Fax: (800) 556-5112
Founded 1978 (1981/2001). Courses in
bookkeeping and accounting; computer-
ized, legal, and medical secretarial skills;
and medical office administration.

National Genealogical Society
(703) 525-0050
4527 Seventeenth St. N
Arlington, VA 22207-2399
Fax: (703) 525-0052
e-mail: 76702.2417@compuserve.com
Internet: http://genealogy.org/NGS/
Founded 1903 (1996/2000). Course in
American genealogical research.

National Institute for Paralegal Arts
and Sciences
164 W. Royal Palm Rd.
Boca Raton, FL 33432
(800) 669-2555
e-mail: nipas@ix.netcom.com
Internet: http://law.net/nipas/index.htm
Founded 1976 (1992/97). Paralegal
specialized associate degree program,
paralegal diploma program, and paralegal
specialty courses.

The National Institute of Nutritional
Education
1010 S. Joliet, Ste. 107
Aurora, CO 80012
(800) 530-8079
Fax: (303) 367-2577
e-mail: nuted@aol.com
Founded 1980 (1996/2001). Certificate
program in nutrition sciences.

National Tax Training School
4 Melnick Dr.
PO Box 382
Monsey, NY 10952
(800) 914-8138
e-mail: ntts@concentric.net
Internet: http://www.nattax.com
Founded 1952 (1965/96). Basic and
advanced federal income tax preparation
courses.

National Training, Inc.
188 College Dr.
PO Box 1899
Orange Park, FL 32067-1899
(904) 272-4000
Founded 1978 (1982/97). Combination
distance study-resident courses in truck-
driver training.

NHRAW Home Study Institute
1389 Dublin Rd.
PO Box 16790
Columbus, OH 43216
(614) 488-1835
Founded 1962 (1969/2000). Not-for-profit
industry program. Courses in
heating, air conditioning, and financial
management for contractors.

NRI Schools
4401 Connecticut Ave. NW
Washington, DC 20008
(202) 244-1600
Fax: (202) 244-2047
e-mail: infor@mhcec.com
A division of McGraw-Hill Companies.
Founded 1914 (1956/97). Associate of
applied science degree programs in
accounting and business management,
and nondegree courses in computers, electronics, programming, networking, automotive technology, air conditioning,
construction, home inspection, computer-
aided drafting, small-engine repair, bookkeeping, paralegal services, fiction and
nonfiction writing, gunsmithing, desktop
publishing, and word processing.

Paralegal Institute, Inc.
3602 W. Thomas Rd., Ste. 9
Drawer 11408
Phoenix, AZ 85061-1408
(800) 354-1254
Founded 1974 (1979/98). Legal assistant
and paralegal training, bookkeeping and
accounting, medical transcription, and
personal computer use. Certification programs for legal assistants. Associate degree
in paralegal studies.

Peoples College
233 Academy Dr.
PO Box 421768
Kissimmee, FL 347442-1768
(407) 847-4444
Fax: (407) 847-8793
A division of Southeastern Academy, Inc.
Founded 1985. Specialized associate de-
grees in travel and tourism management,
personal computer programming, elec-

tronics technology with PC servicing, and
industrial controls or communications
specializations. Nondegree programs in
communication electronics with microprocessor technology, computer servicing
and electronics technology, industrial
electronics and microprocessor technology, personal computer programming,
and business computing. Avocational
program in powerboat handling and
seamanship.

Professional Career Development
Institute
3597 Parkway La., Ste. 100
Norcross, GA 30092
(800) 362-7070
Founded 1987 (1993/97). Courses in
paralegal services, bookkeeping and accounting, animal care, interior decorating,
VCR repair, travel, gunsmithing, personal
computer, hotel and restaurant management, medical and dental office assisting,
home inspection, PC repair, fitness and
nutrition, auto mechanics, medical and
legal transcription, conservation, floral
design, electricity, tax preparation, motor-
cycle repair, locksmithing, day care for
children, and computer applications.
High school studies also available.

Richard M. Milburn High School
14416 Jefferson Davis Hwy., Ste. 12
Woodbridge, VA 22191
(703) 494-0147
Founded 1975 (1994/98). Courses in full
four-year high-school diploma program.
Spanish, Saudi Arabic, and German
Headstart courses.

Seminary Extension Independent Study
Institute
901 Commerce St., St. 500
Nashville, TN 37203-3631
(615) 242-2453
Fax: (615) 782-4822
e-mail: 104072.3410.compuserve.com
Founded 1951 (1972/97). Courses in
Bible, Christian doctrine, Christian
history, religious education, and pastor
ministries.

Southeastern Academy, Inc.
233 Academy Dr.
PO Box 421768
Kissimmee, FL 34742-1768
(407) 847-4444
Fax: (407) 847-8793
Founded 1974 (1977/97). Combination
distance study-resident courses in airline,
travel agency, hotel, and car rental services.

Stenotype Institute of Jacksonville, Inc.
500 Ninth Ave. N
PO Box 50009
Jacksonville Beach, FL 32250
(904) 246-7466
Fax: (904) 246-0129
Founded 1940 (1987/96). Course in court
reporting, using stenotype machine short-
hand, and computer-aided transcription.

Trans World Travel Academy
Charles A. Lindbergh Training Center
11495 Natural Bridge Rd.
St. Louis, MO 63044-9842
Founded 1978 (1981/97). Combination
distance study-resident courses in airline,
flight attendant, and travel agent career
training.

Truck Marketing Institute
1090 Eugenia Pl.
PO Box 5000
Carpinteria, CA 93014-5000
(805) 684-4558
Founded 1964 (1968/99). Courses in
truck selection, application, and sales.

U.S. Coast Guard Institute
5900 S.W. 64th St., Rm. 235
Oklahoma City, OK 73169-6990
(405) 954-4262
Fax: (405) 954-7249
e-mail: cglearn~ionet.net
Internet: http://www.productive.com *and*
http://USCGVolE@ionet.net
Founded 1928 (1981/2001). U.S. Coast
Guard military and technical training
courses. Enrollment restricted to active-
duty and reserve military, Coast Guard
auxiliarists, retired Coast Guard personnel, civilian employees of the Coast
Guard, and commissioned officers of
the National Oceanic and Atmospheric
Administration.

Westlawn Institute of Marine
Technology
733 Summer St.
Stamford, CT 06901
(203) 359-0500
Founded 1930 (1971/96). Courses in
boat and yacht design and related marine
technology subjects.

World College
Lake Shores Plaza
5193 Shore Dr., Ste. 113
Virginia Beach, VA 23455-2500
(804) 464-4600
Founded 1992 (1993/97). Bachelor of
electronic engineering technology.

# State Resources
# for Small Business

There is usually a primary state government agency or office in each state that provides one-stop guidance on the programs and services available to small businesses. Note that all programs and offices listed for a particular state are not necessarily part of the primary office, which is listed first.

*Business Development* offers start-up information on regulatory laws and permits; location selection assistance, demographic information; management training; bookkeeping; employee benefits and payroll administration; money management; technical and manufacturing assistance; labor and personnel training and high technology development.

*Financial Assistance* provides information on guaranteed, direct, and revolving loans; grants; revenue bonds; information on venture capital sources and tax incentives.

*Minority/Women's Opportunities* provides programs targeted to small businesses owned and operated by minorities and women. While programs vary by state, most offer assistance with government contracting, training, and business development and financing, either through intermediaries or by acting as a clearinghouse for sources of financial assistance.

*Small Business Development Centers* offer counseling, workshops, and resource material for start-up and ongoing small-business ventures.

*Other State Resources* includes addresses and phone numbers of selected federal, state, and private sector organizations in that state.

The Small Business Administration's Office of Advocacy publishes a book called *The States and Small Business: A Directory of Programs and Activities* (GPO stock number 045-000-00266-7), which gives more details on many of the programs and services listed here. To order a copy, call the Government Printing Office, (202) 512-1800.

## ALABAMA

Alabama Development Office
401 Adams Ave.
Montgomery, AL 36130-4106
(334) 242-0400

### Business Development

Alabama Small Business Development
Consortium
(205) 934-7260
Small Business Office of Advocacy
(334) 242-0400

### Financial Assistance

Economic Development Administration
(334) 223-7008

### Minority/Women's Opportunities

Office of Minority Business Enterprise
(334) 242-2220

### Small Business Development Centers

University of Alabama at Birmingham
1717 11th Ave. S, Ste. 419
Birmingham, AL 35294
(205) 934-6760

Auburn; (334) 844-4220

Florence; (205) 760-4624

Huntsville; (205) 535-2061

Jacksonville; (205) 782-5271

Mobile; (334) 460-6004

Montgomery; (334) 229-4138

Troy; (334) 670-3771

Tuscaloosa, (University of Alabama)
(205) 348-7011

### Other Alabama Resources

Business Council of Alabama
2 N. Jackson St.
PO Box 76
Montgomery, AL 36101
(334) 834-6000

Small Business Administration
District Office
2121 Eighth Ave. N, Ste. 200
Birmingham, AL 35203-2398
(205) 731-1344

U.S. Dept. of Commerce District Office
960 Twenty-second St. N, Rm. 707
Birmingham, AL 35203-0131
(205) 731-1331

Internal Revenue Service
(800) 829-1040

## ALASKA

Dept. of Commerce and Economic
Development
State Office Bldg., 9th Fl.
333 Willoughby Ave.
PO Box 110800
Juneau, AK 99811-0800
(907) 465-2500

### Business Development

Division of Trade and Development
(907) 465-2017

Business Development Information
Network
(907) 465-3961

Economic Development, Fairbanks
Native Association, Inc.
(907) 452-1648

**Financial Assistance**

Division of Trade and Development
(907) 465-2017

Division of Investments: Commercial
Fishing Loan Program, Small Business
Economic Development Revolving
Loan Fund
(907) 465-2510

Alaska Industrial Development and
Export Authority: Loan Participation Program, Development Finance Program,
Small Business Economic Development
Revolving Loan Fund
(907) 269-3000

**Minority/Women's Opportunities**

Alaska Business Development Center
(907) 562-0335 or (800) 478-3474

Minority Business Development Center
(907) 274-5400

**Rural Development**

Division of Community and Rural
Development
(907) 465-5539

Dept. of Natural Resources: Division
of Agriculture, Wholesale Agricultural
Market Development, Alaska State
Agricultural Loan Program
(907) 745-7200

**Publication**

*Economic Development Resource Guide*
(907) 465-5543

**Small Business Development Centers**

University of Alaska at Anchorage
430 W. Seventh Ave., Ste. 110
Anchorage, AK 99501
(907) 274-7232

Fairbanks; (907) 474-6400

Juneau; (907) 463-3789

Kenai; (907) 283-3335

Wasilla; (907) 373-7232

**Other Alaska Resources**

Alaska State Chamber of Commerce
217 Second St., Ste. 201
Juneau, AK 99801
(907) 586-2323

Small Business Administration
District Office
222 W. Eighth Ave., Rm. A-36
PO Box 67
Anchorage, AK 99513-7559
(907) 271-4022

U.S. Dept. of Commerce District Office;
421 W. First Ave., Ste. 300
Anchorage, AK 99501-1635
(907) 271-6237

Internal Revenue Service
(800) 829-1040

## ARIZONA

Business Development Finance Corp.
186 E. Broadway Blvd.
Tucson, AZ 85701
(800) 264-3377

### Business Development

Arizona Small Business Development
Center Network
(602) 731-8720

Arizona Business Connection
(602) 280-1480 *or* (800) 542-5684

Business Retention and Expansion
(602) 280-1350

Commerce and Economic Development
Commission
(602) 280-1341

### Financial Assistance

Business Development Finance Corp.
(800) 264-3377

Small Business Financing Programs
(602) 280-1341

### Small Business Development Centers:

Arizona Small Business Development
Center Network
2411 W. 14th St., Rm. 132
Tempe, AZ 85281
(602) 731-8720

Coolidge; (520) 426-4341

Flagstaff; (520) 526-5072

Kingman; (520) 757-0894

Nogales; (520) 287-2569

Payson; (520) 474-8821

Phoenix (Greater Maricopa County);
(602) 392-5223

Prescott; (520) 778-3088

Show Low; (800) 266-7232

Sierra Vista; (520) 515-5478

Thatcher; (520) 428-8590

Tucson; (520) 748-4906

Yuma; (520) 341-1650

### Other Arizona Resources

Arizona Chamber of Commerce
1221 E. Osborn Rd., Ste. 100
Phoenix, AZ 85014
(602) 248-9172

Small Business Administration
District Office
2828 N. Central Ave., Ste. 800
Phoenix, AZ 85004-1093
(602) 640-2513

U.S. Dept. of Commerce District Office
2901 N. Central Ave., Ste. 970
Phoenix, AZ 85012-2793

Internal Revenue Service
(800) 829-1040

## ARKANSAS

Arkansas Industrial Development
Commission
One State Capitol Mall
Little Rock, AR 72201
(501) 682-1121

### Business Development

Advocacy
(501) 682-7325

The Arkansas Science and
Technology Authority
(501) 324-9006

Census and Demographic Data
(501) 569-8530

Cooperative Extension Service
(501) 671-2000

Established Industries
(501) 682-7315

General Business Assistance (SCORE)
(501) 324-5893

Genesis Technology Business Incubator
(501) 575-7227

Industrial Development
(501) 682-7675

Small Business Programs
(501) 682-7782

### Financial Assistance

Arkansas Capital Corp.
(501) 374-9247

Bond Guaranty Program
(501) 682-7682

### Minority/Women's Opportunities

Minority Business Development
Program
(501) 682-1060

### Rural Development

Rural Advocacy
(501) 682-6011

### Small Business Development Centers

University of Arkansas at Little Rock
100 S. Main St., Ste. 401
Little Rock, AR 72201
(501) 324-9043

Arkadelphia; (501) 230-5224

Fayetteville; (501) 575-5148

Ft. Smith; (501) 785-1376

Harrison; (501) 741-8009

Hot Springs; (501) 624-5448

Magnolia; (501) 234-4030

Pine Bluff; (501) 536-0654

State University; (501) 972-3517

Stuttgart; (501) 673-8707

West Memphis; (501) 733-6767

## Other Arkansas Resources

Arkansas State Chamber of Commerce
410 Cross St.
PO Box 3645
Little Rock, AR 77203
(501) 374-9225

Small Business Administration
District Office
2120 Riverfront Dr., Ste. 100
Little Rock, AR 72201-3439
(501) 324-5871

Internal Revenue Service
(800) 829-1040

## CALIFORNIA

California Office of Small Business
California Trade and Commerce Agency
801 K St., Ste. 1700
Sacramento, CA 95814
(916) 324-1295

### Business Development

Small Business Development Centers
(916) 324-5068

Office of Business Development
(916) 322-3520

Office of Economic Research
(916) 324-5853

Office of Small Business
(916) 324-1295

Small Business Helpline
(916) 327-4357

### Financial Assistance

Small Business Loan Guarantee Program
(916) 324-1295

### International Trade

California Office of Export Finance
(714) 562-5519

### Minority/Women's Opportunities

Office of Small and Minority Business
(916) 322-5060

### Rural Development

Rural Economic Development
Infrastructure Program
(916) 322-1498

### Small Business Development Centers

California Trade and Commerce Agency
801 K St., Ste. 1700
Sacramento, CA 95814-3520
(916) 324-5068

Aptos; (408) 479-6136

Auburn; (916) 885-5488

Bakersfield; (805) 322-5881

Chico; (916) 895-9017

Chula Vista; (619) 482-6391

Clearlake; (707) 995-3440

Crescent City; (707) 464-2168

Eureka; (707) 445-9720

Fresno; (209) 275-1223

Gilroy; (408) 847-0373

Irvine; (714) 509-2990

La Jolla; (619) 453-9388

Los Angeles (ITC); (213) 892-1111

Los Angeles (South Central)
(213) 846-1710

Merced; (209) 725-3800

Modesto; (209) 521-6177

Napa; (707) 253-3210

Oakland; (510) 893-4114

Oxnard; (805) 644-6191

Palm Springs; (619) 864-1311

Pasadena; (818) 398-9031

Pomona; (909) 629-2247

Riverside; (909) 781-2345

Sacramento; (916) 563-3210

Santa Ana; (714) 647-1172

Santa Monica; (310) 398-8883

Santa Rosa; (707) 524-1770

Stockton; (209) 474-5089

Suisun;(707) 864-3382

Torrance; (310) 787-6466

Van Nuys; (818) 373-7092

Ventura; (805) 658-2688

Visalia; (209) 625-3051

### Other California Resources

California Chamber of Commerce
1201 K St., 12th Fl.
PO Box 1736
Sacramento, CA 95812
(916) 444-6670

Small Business Administration
District Offices
2719 N. Air Fresno Dr., Ste. 107
Fresno, CA 93727-1547
(209) 487-5189

330 N. Brand Blvd., Ste. 1200
Glendale, CA 91203-2304
(818) 552-3210

660 J St., Ste. 215
Sacramento, CA 95814-2413
(916) 498-6410

200 W. Santa Ana Blvd., Ste. 700
Santa Ana, CA 92701
(714) 550-7420

550 West C St., Ste. 550
San Diego, CA 92101
(619) 557-5440

211 Main St., 4th Fl.
San Francisco, CA 94105-1988
(415) 744-6820

U.S. Dept. of Commerce District Offices
11000 Wilshire Blvd., Rm. 9200
Los Angeles, CA 90024-3611
(310) 235-7104

One World Trade Center, Ste. 1670
Long Beach, CA 90831
(310) 235-7104

3300 Irvine Ave., Ste. 305
Newport Beach, CA 92660-3108
(714) 660-1688

6363 Greenwich Dr., Ste. 230
San Diego, CA 92122-5947
(619) 557-5395

250 Montgomery St., 14th Fl.
San Francisco, CA 94104-3401
(415) 705-2300

Internal Revenue Service
(800) 829-1040

## COLORADO

Office of Business Development
1625 Broadway, Ste. 1710
Denver, CO 80202
(303) 892-3840

### Business Development

Colorado Dept. of Labor and
Employment
(303) 620-4701

Colorado FIRST Customized
Training Program
(303) 892-3840

Office of Regulatory Reform
(303) 894-7839

Office of Certification
(303) 894-2355

Business Assistance
(303) 592-5920 *or* (800) 333-7798

### Financial Assistance

Colorado Agricultural Development
Authority
(303) 239-4117

Colorado Housing and Finance Authority
(303) 297-2432

Office of Business Development,
Finance Division
(303) 892-3840

### Minority/Women's Opportunities

Minority Business Office
(303) 892-3840

Women's Business Office
(303) 892-3840

### Small Business Development Centers

Office of Business Development
Colorado Small Business Development
Center, 1625 Broadway, Ste. 1710
Denver, CO 80202
(303) 892-3809

Alamosa; (719) 589-7372

Aurora; (303) 341-4849

Colorado Springs; (719) 592-1894

Craig; (970) 824-7078

Delta; (970) 874-8772

Denver; (303) 620-8076

Durango; (970) 247-7009

Ft. Collins; (970) 226-0881

Ft. Morgan; (970) 867-3351

Glenwood Springs; (800) 621-1647

Grand Junction; (970) 243-5242

Greeley; (970) 352-3661

Lakewood; (303) 987-0710

Lamar; (719) 336-8141

Littleton; (303) 795-0142

Pueblo; (719) 549-3224

Trinidad; (719) 846-5645

Westminster; (303) 460-1032

### Other Colorado Resources

Colorado Association of Commerce
and Industry
1776 Lincoln St., Ste. 1200
Denver, CO 80203
(303) 831-7411

Small Business Administration
District Office
721 Nineteenth St., Ste. 426
Denver, CO 80202-2599
(303) 844-3984

U.S. Dept. of Commerce District Office
1625 Broadway, St. 680
Denver, CO 80202-4706
(303) 844-6622

Internal Revenue Service
Denver; (303) 825-7041
Elsewhere; (800) 829-1040

## CONNECTICUT

Office of Small Business Services
Dept. of Economic and Community
Development
865 Brook St.
Rocky Hill, CT 06067-34056
(860) 258-4200
http://www.cerc.com

### Business Development

One-Stop Business Registry
(800) 392-2122

Connecticut Innovations: R&D, technology transfer, manufacturing applications;
(800) 392-2122

Office of Business Ombudsman
(860) 258-4200

Project Management: guiding through
state, regional, and local economic
development agencies
(800) 392-2122

Tax Abatements; manufacturing equipment and machinery, repair and replacement parts, computer and data processing
equipment

(800) 392-2122

Connecticut State Technology Extension Program (CONN/STEP): needs assessments, training, skills development
(800) 392-2122

Center for Flexible Manufacturing Networks: strategic partnerships, technical support, network training and management, financial packaging
(800) 392-2122

## Financial Assistance

Connecticut Development Authority
(800) 392-2122

Manufacturing Assistance: tax credits, loan guarantees, investment, and direct loans
(800) 392-2122

Connecticut Works Fund: loan guarantees, direct loans
(800) 392-2122

Connecticut Innovations, Inc.: early-stage financing for high-tech companies
(800) 392-2122

## Minority/Women's Assistance

Urban lending
(800) 392-2122

## Small Business Development Centers

University of Connecticut
School of Business Administration
2 Bourn Pl., U-94

Storrs, CT 06269-5094
(203) 486-4135

Bridgeport; (203) 330-4813

Danbury; (203) 743-5565

Danielson; (203) 774-1133

Groton; (203) 449-1188

Middletown; (203) 344-2158

New Haven; (203) 782-4390

Stamford; (203) 359-3220, ext. 302

Waterbury; (203) 757-8937

West Hartford; (203) 241-4986

Willimantic; (860) 465-5349

## Other Connecticut Resources

Connecticut Business and Industry Association
370 Asylum St.
Hartford, CT 061103
(860) 244-1900

Small Business Administration
District Office
330 Main St., 2nd Fl.
Hartford, CT 06106
(860) 240-4700

U.S. Dept. of Commerce District Office
213 Court St.
Middletown, CT 06457
(860) 638-6950

Internal Revenue Service
(800) 829-1040

## DELAWARE

Delaware Economic Development Office
99 Kings Hwy.
PO Box 1401
Dover, DE 19903
(302) 739-4271
http://www.de.state.us/govern/agencies/
dedo/index.htm

### Business Development

Business Development
(302) 739-4271

Business Research
(302) 739-4271

Education, Training, and Recruitment
(302) 739-4271

Small Business Advocate
(302) 739-4271

### Financial Assistance

Business Finance: Small Business Revolving Loan and Credit Enhancement Fund
(302) 739-4271

Delaware Economic Development
Authority
(302) 739-4271

### Small Business Development Centers

University of Delaware
Purnell Hall, Ste. 005
Newark, DE 19716-2711
(302) 831-1555 *or* (800) 222-2279

Dover; (302) 678-1555

Georgetown; (302) 856-1555

### Other Delaware Resources

Delaware State Chamber of Commerce
1201 N. Orange St., Ste. 200
PO Box 671
Wilmington, DE 19899
(302) 655-7221

Small Business`Administration
Branch Office
824 N. Market St., Ste. 610
Wilmington, DE 19801-3011
(302) 573-6294

U.S. Dept. of Commerce District Office
615 Chestnut St., Ste. 1501
Philadelphia, PA 19106
(215) 597-6101

Internal Revenue Service
(800) 829-1040

## DISTRICT OF COLUMBIA

Office of Economic Development
717 14th St. NW, 12th Fl.
Washington, DC 20005
(202) 727-6600

## Business Development

Business and Permit Center
(202) 727-7100

Dept. of Consumer and Regulatory
Affairs
(202) 727-7000

Incorporation/Corporate Division
(202) 727-7278

## Financial Assistance

Economic Development Finance Corp.
(202) 775-8815

Industrial Revenue Bond Program
(202) 727-6600

Loan Guarantee Program
(202) 535-1942

## Minority/Women's Opportunities

Dept. of Human Rights and Minority
Business Development
(202) 724-1385

Washington, DC, Minority Business
Development Center
(202) 785-2886

Procurement (Dept. of Administrative
Services)
(202) 727-0252

## Small Business Development Centers

Metropolitan Washington Small Business
Development Center
Howard University
2600 Sixth St. NW, Rm. 125
Washington, DC 20059
(202) 806-1550

Development Corp. of Columbia Heights
(202) 483-4986

East of the River Community
Development Corp.
(202) 561-4975

Small Business Administration
Information Center
(202) 606-4000 x279

George Washington University
Small Business Clinic
(202) 994-7463

Marshall Heights Community
Development Organization
(202) 396-1200

## Other Washington, DC, Resources

District of Columbia Chamber of
Commerce
(202) 638-3222

Small Business Administration
District Office
1110 Vermont Ave. NW, Ste. 900
Washington, DC 20043-4500
(202) 606-4000

U.S. Dept. of Commerce District Office
700 Center, 704 E. Franklin St., Ste. 550
Richmond, VA 23219
(804) 771-2246

Internal Revenue Service
(800) 829-1040

### FLORIDA

Enterprise Florida
Suntrust Center
200 S. Orange Ave., Ste. 1200
Orlando, FL 32801
(407) 425-5313

#### Business Development

Technology Division
(407) 425-5313

Workforce Division
(904) 921-1119

Tourism, Trade and Economic
Development
(904) 487-2568

International Trade Division
(305) 870-5000

Manufacturing Technology Division
(954) 941-0115

#### Financial Assistance

Capital Division
(407) 425-5313

Grant Division
(904) 488-6300

#### Minority/Women's Opportunities

Enterprise Florida
(407) 425-5313

#### Small Business Development Centers

University of West Florida
19 West Garden Street, Suite 300
Pensacola, FL 32501
(904) 444-2060

Boca Raton; (561) 362-5620

Dania; (954) 987-0100

Daytona Beach; (904) 947-5463

Fort Lauderdale; (954) 771-6520

Fort Myers; (941) 489-9200

Fort Pierce; (561) 462-4756

Fort Walton Beach; (904) 863-6543

Gainesville (CDC); (352) 377-5621

Jacksonville; (904) 646-2476

Lynn Haven; (904) 271-1108

Melbourne; (407) 632-1111 ext. 32760

Miami; (Miami Dade); (305) 237-1900

Miami (Florida International University);
(305) 348-2272

Ocala; (352) 629-8051

Orlando; (407) 823-5554

Pensacola (Pensacola Tech.);
(904) 444-2066

Pensacola (University of Western
Florida);
(904) 474-2908

Sanford; (407) 834-4404

St. Petersburg; (813) 341-4456

Tallahassee; (904) 599-3407

Tampa (University of Southern Florida);
(813) 554-2341

**Other Florida Resources**

Florida Chamber of Commerce
136 S. Bronough St.
Tallahassee, FL 32302
(904) 425-1200

Small Business Administration
District Offices
1320 S. Dixie Hwy., Ste. 301
Coral Gables, FL 33146-2911
(305) 536-5521

7825 Baymeadows Way, Ste. 100B
Jacksonville, FL 32256-7504
(904) 443-1900

U.S. Dept. of Commerce District Offices
128 North Osceola Ave.
P.O. Box 2457
Clearwater, FL 34617-2456
(813) 461-0011

5600 N.W. 36th St., Ste. 617
PO Box 590670
Miami, FL 33159
(305) 526-7425

Collins Bldg.
107 W. Gaines St. Rm. G-01
Tallahassee, FL 32399
(904) 488-6469

Internal Revenue Service
Jacksonville; (904) 354-1760
Elsewhere; (800) 829-1040

### GEORGIA

Georgia Dept. of Industry,
Trade and Tourism
PO Box 1776
Atlanta, GA 30301
(404) 656-3545

**Business Development**

Small Business Revitalization Program
(404) 656-3872

Business Development Corp. of Georgia
(404) 656-3556

**Financial Assistance**

Dept. of Industry, Trade, and Tourism
(404) 656-3556

**Minority/Women's Opportunities**

Office of Small and Minority Affairs
(404) 656-6315

**Rural Development**

Office of Rural Development
(404) 656-5525

## Small Business Development Centers

University of Georgia
Business Outreach Services
Chicopee Complex
1180 E. Broad St.
Athens, GA 30602-5412
(706) 542-6762

Albany; (912) 430-4303

Athens (N.E. District); (706) 542-7436
(N.W. District); (706) 542-6756

Atlanta (Georgia State University);
(404) 651-3550

Atlanta (University of Atlanta);
(404) 220-0205

Augusta; (706) 737-1790

Brunswick; (912) 264-7343

Columbus; (706) 649-7433

Decatur; (404) 373-6930

Gainesville; (770) 531-5681

Lawrenceville; (770) 806-2124

Macon; (912) 751-6592

Marietta; (770) 423-3440

Morrow; (770) 961-3440

Rome; (706) 295-6326

Statesboro; (912) 681-5194

Valdosta; (912) 245-3738

Warner Robbins; (912) 953-9356

## Other Georgia Resources

Georgia Chamber of Commerce
233 Peachtree St., Ste. 200
Atlanta, GA 30303
(404) 223-2264

Small Business Administration
District Office
1720 Peachtree Rd. NW, Ste. 600
Atlanta, GA 30309
(404) 347-2441

U.S. Dept. of Commerce District Offices
285 Peachtree Center Ave. NE, Ste. 200
Atlanta, GA 30303-1229
(404) 657-1900

120 Barnard St., Rm. A-107
Savannah, GA 31401-3645
(912) 652-4204

Internal Revenue Service
Atlanta; (404) 522-0050
Elsewhere; (800) 829-1040

## HAWAII

Dept. of Business, Economic
Development and Tourism
250 S. Hotel St., 5th Fl.
Honolulu, HI 96813
(808) 586-2591

## Business Development

Business Action Center
(808) 586-2545

Pacific Business Center
(808) 956-6286

Business Information and Counseling
Center
(808) 522-8131

SBA-SCORE/ACE
(808) 541-2977

## Financial Assistance

Financial Assistance Branch
(808) 586-2576

Agricultural Loan Division
(808) 973-9460

## Minority/Women's Opportunities

Women in Business Committee
(808) 541-3024

## Rural Development

Cooperative Extension Service
(808) 244-3242

## Small Business Development Centers

University of Hawaii at Hilo
200 West Kawili St.
Hilo, HI 96720-4091
(808) 933-3515

Honolulu; (808) 522-8131

Kihei; (808) 875-2402

Lihue; (808) 246-1748

## Other Hawaii Resources

The Chamber of Commerce of Hawaii
1132 Bishop St., Ste. 200
Honolulu, HI 96813
(808) 545-4300

Small Business Administration
District Office
200 Ala Moana Blvd., Rm. 2213
Honolulu, HI 96850-4981
(808) 541-2990

U.S. Dept. of Commerce District Office
300 Ala Moana Blvd., Rm. 4106
PO Box 50026
Honolulu, HI 96850
(808) 541-1782

Internal Revenue Service
(800) 829-1040

# IDAHO

Dept. of Commerce
700 W. State St.
PO Box 83720
Boise, ID 83720-2700
(208) 334-2470

## Business Development

Division of Economic Development
(208) 334-2470

Idaho Business Network
(208) 334-2470

**Financial Assistance**

Pan Handle Area Council
Business Center for Innovation
and Development
(208) 772-0584

Idaho Innovation Center
(208) 523-1026

**Minority/Women's Opportunities**

Associated General Contractors
of America
(208) 344-2531

**Rural Development**

Idaho Rural Development Council
(208) 344-6184

**Small Business Development Centers**

Boise State University
College of Business
1910 University Dr.
Boise, ID 83725
(208) 385-1640 *or*
(800) 225-3815 (in Idaho)

Idaho Falls; (208) 523-1087

Lewiston; (208) 799-2465

Pocatello; (208) 232-4921

Post Falls; (208) 769-3296

Twin Falls; (208) 733-9554, ext. 2450

**Other Idaho Resources**

Idaho Association of Commerce
and Industry
6802 W. Bannock St., Ste. 308
PO Box 389
Boise, ID 83701
(208) 343-1849

Small Business Administration
District Office
1020 Main St., Ste. 290
Boise, ID 83702-5745
(208) 334-1696

U.S. Dept. of Commerce District Office
700 W. State St.
PO Box 83720
Boise, ID 83720-0093
(208) 334-2470

Internal Revenue Service
(800) 829-1040

## ILLINOIS

Small Business Development Center Dept.
of Commerce and Community Affairs
620 E. Adams St., 3rd Fl.
Springfield, IL 62701
(217) 524-5856

**Business Development**

Illinois First-Stop Program
(800) 252-2923 (in Illinois)

Illinois Business Hotline
(800) 252-2923 (in Illinois)

Illinois Small Business Development
Center Network
(800) 252-2923 (in Illinois)

Small Business Environmental
Assistance
(800) 252-3998 (in Illinois)

### Financial Assistance

Loan Administration Division
Chicago; (312) 814-2308

Springfield; (217) 782-38891

### Minority/Women's Opportunities

Office of Minority Business
Development
(312) 814-3540

Office of Women's Business
Development
(312) 814-7176

### Small Business Development Centers

Department of Commerce and
Community Affairs
620 E. Adams St., 3rd Fl.
Springfield, IL 62701
(217) 524-5856

Chicago Asian American Alliance
(312) 202-0600

Back of the Yards Neighborhood Council
(312) 523-4419

DCAA State of Illinois Center
(312) 814-6111

18th Street Development Corp.
(312) 733-2287

Greater North Pulaski Economic

Development Council
(312) 384-2262

Industrial Council
(312) 421-3941

Latin American Chamber of Commerce
(312) 252-5211

New Business and Industrial Council
(312) 588-5855

Women's Business Development
(312) 853-3477

Aurora; (630) 892-3334, ext. 1139

Carbondale; (618) 536-2424

Centralia; (618) 532-2049

Chicago; (312) 853-3477

Crystal Lake; (815) 455-6098

Danville; (217) 442-7232

Decatur; (217) 875-8284

Dixon; (815) 288-5605

East Moline; (309) 752-9759, ext. 211

East St. Louis; (618) 482-3833

Edwardsville; (618) 692-2929

Elgin; (847) 888-7675

Evanston; (847) 866-1817

Glen Ellyn; (630) 858-2800, ext. 2771

Godfrey; (618) 467-2370

Grayslake; (847) 223-3633

Harrisburg; (618) 252-5001

Ina; (618) 437-5321, ext. 335

Joliet; (815) 727-6544, ext. 1400

Kankakee; (815) 933-0376

Macomb; (309) 298-2211

Monmouth; (309) 734-4664

Oglesby; (815) 223-1740

Olney; (618) 395-3011

Palos Hills; (708) 974-5468

Peoria; (309) 677-2992

Quincy; (217) 228-5511

River Grove; (708) 456-0300, ext. 3593

Rockford; (815) 968-4087

Springfield; (217) 789-1017

Ullin; (618) 634-9618

University Park; (708) 534-4929

### Other Illinois Resources

The Illinois State Chamber of Commerce
311 S. Wacker Dr., Ste. 1500
Chicago, IL 60606-6619
(312) 983-7100

Small Business Administration
District Offices
500 W. Madison St., Rm. 1250
Chicago, IL 60661-2511
(312) 353-4528
511 W. Capitol Ave., Ste. 302
Springfield, IL 62704
(217) 492-4401

U.S. Dept. of Commerce District Offices
55 W. Monroe St., Ste. 2440
Chicago, IL 60603-5008
(312) 353-8040
515 N. Court St.
Rockford, IL 61103-0247
(815) 987-8123

Illinois Institute of Technology
Rice Campus, 201 E. Loop R
Wheaton, IL 60187-8488
(312) 353-4332

Internal Revenue Service
(800) 929-1040

### INDIANA

State Information Center
402 W. Washington St., Rm. W160
Indianapolis, IN 46204
(317) 233-0800
(800) 45-STATE (in Indiana)

### Business Development

Indiana Dept. of Commerce
(317) 232-8800

Indiana Administrative Services Division
(317) 232-8782

Business Development Division
(317) 232-8888

Indiana Business Modernization
and Technology Corp.
(317) 635-3058

Indiana Small Business
Development Corp.
(317) 264-2820

Indiana Small Business Development
Centers
(317) 264-6871

### Financial Assistance

Indiana Development Finance Authority
(317) 233-4332

### Minority/Women's Opportunities

Women and Minority Business
Assistance Program
(317) 264-2820

Minority Business Development
Division
(317) 232-3061

### Rural Development

Indiana Commission for Agriculture and
Rural Development
(317) 232-8770

### Small Business Development Centers

Indiana Small Business
Development Center
One N. Capitol, Ste. 420
Indianapolis, IN 46204-2248
(317) 264-6871

Bloomington; (812) 339-8937

Columbus; (812) 372-6480

Evansville; (812) 425-7232

Ft. Wayne; (219) 426-0040

Indianapolis; (317) 261-3030

Jeffersonville; (812) 288-6451

Kokomo; (317) 454-7922

Lafayette; (317) 742-2394

Madison; (812) 265-3127

Muncie; (317) 284-8144

Portage; (219) 762-1696

Richmond; (317) 962-2887

South Bend; (219) 282-4350

Terre Haute; (812) 237-7676

### Other Indiana Resources

Indiana State Chamber of
Commerce, Inc.
One N. Capitol St., Ste. 200
Indianapolis, IN 46204-2248
(317) 264-3110

Small Business Administration
District Office
429 N. Pennsylvania, Ste. 100
Indianapolis, IN 46204-1873
(317) 226-7272

U.S. Dept. of Commerce District Office
11405 N. Pennsylvania St., St. 106
Carmel, IN 46032-6905
(317) 582-2300

Internal Revenue Service
(800) 829-1040

## IOWA

Dept. of Economic Development
200 E. Grand Ave.
Des Moines, IA 50309
(515) 242-4700

### Business Development

Center for Industrial Research
and Service
(515) 294-3420

Marketing and Business Expansion
Bureau
(515) 242-4735

Office of Ombudsman
(515) 281-3592

Small Business Bureau
(515) 242-4750

Small Business Helpline
(800) 532-1216

Small Business Workforce Development
(515) 281-9013

### Financial Assistance

Economic Development Set-Aside
(515) 242-4831

Iowa Seed Capital Corp.
(515) 242-4860

### Minority/Women's Opportunities

Targeted Small Business Bond Waiver
Program; (515) 281-7250

Linked Investments for Tomorrow
Program
(515) 281-3287

Targeted Small Business Financial
Assistance Program
(515) 242-4813

Targeted Small Business Program
(515) 242-4721

Entrepreneurs with Disabilities Program
(515) 242-4948

Self-Employment Loan Program
(515) 242-4793

### Rural Development

Rural Development Program
(515) 242-4840

Value-Added Agricultural Products
and Processes
(515) 242-4801

### Small Business Development Centers

Iowa State University
College of Business Administration
137 Lynn Ave., Ames, IA50014-7126
(515) 292-6351, *or*
(800) 373-7232 (in Iowa)

Ames; (515) 296-7828

Audubon; (712) 563-2623

Cedar Falls; (319) 273-2696

Council Bluffs; (712) 325-3260

Creston; (515) 782-4161

Davenport; (319) 322-4499

Des Moines; (515) 271-2655

Dubuque; (319) 588-3350

Ft. Dodge; (800) 362-2793, ext. 2730

Iowa City; (319) 335-3742

Marion; (319) 377-8256

Mason City; (515) 422-342

Ottumwa; (515) 683-5127

Sioux City; (712) 274-6418

Spencer; (712) 262-4213

West Burlington; (319) 752-2731, ext. 103

## Other Iowa Resources

Iowa Association of Business
and Industry
904 Walnut St., Ste. 100
Des Moines, IA 50309-3503
(515) 244-6149

Small Business Association District Offices
215 Fourth Ave. SE, Ste. 200
Cedar Rapids, IA 52401-1806
(319) 362-6405

210 Walnut St., Rm. 749
Des Moines, IA 50309-2186
(515) 284-4422

U.S. Dept. of Commerce District Office
210 Walnut St., Rm. 817
Des Moines, IA 50309-2105
(515) 284-4222

Internal Revenue Service
Des Moines; (515) 283-0523
Elsewhere; (800) 829-1040

## KANSAS

Dept. of Commerce
700 S.W. Harrison St., Ste. 1300
Topeka, KS 66603-3712
(913) 296-3481

### Business Development

Administration Division
(913) 296-3481

Agriculture Value-Added Processing
Center
(913) 532-7033

Kansas Technology Enterprise Corp.
(913) 296-5272

Kansas Job Training Partnership Act
(913) 296-7876

## Financial Assistance

Certified Development Companies
(316) 683-4422

Power Certified Development
Companies
(316) 267-3036

Kansas Development Finance Authority
(913) 296-6747

Kansas Venture Capital, Inc.
(913) 262-7117

## Minority/Women's Opportunities

Office of Minority Business
(913) 296-1847

## Small Business Development Centers

Wichita State University
1845 Fairmount
Wichita, KS 67260-0148
(316) 978-3193

Achison; (913) 367-5340, 2414

Augusta; (316) 775-1124

Chamite; (316) 431-2820, ext. 266

Coffeyville; (316) 251-7700, ext. 2130

Concordia; (913) 243-1435, ext. 215

Dodge City; (316) 227-9247

Ft. Scott; (316) 223-2700, ext. 89

Garden City; (316) 276-9632

Hays; (913) 628-5340

Hutchinson; (316) 665-4950

Independence; (316) 332-1420

Iola; (316) 365-5116, ext. 218

Lawrence; (913) 843-8844

Liberal; (316) 629-2650

Manhattan; (913) 532-5529

Ottawa; (913) 242-5200, ext. 5457

Overland Park; (913) 469-3878

Parsons; (316) 421-6700, ext. 38

Pittsburg; (316) 235-4920

Pratt; (316) 672-5641, ext. 200

Salina; (913) 826-2616

Topeka; (913) 231-1010, ext. 1305

## Other Kansas Resources

Kansas Chamber of Commerce
and Industry
835 S.W. Topeka Blvd.
Topeka, KS 66612-1671
(913) 357-6321

Small Business Administration
District Office
100 E. English St., Ste. 510
Wichita, KS 67202
(316) 269-6616

Internal Revenue Service
(800) 892-1040

## KENTUCKY

Kentucky Cabinet for Economic
Development
Capital Plaza Tower
Frankfurt, KY 40601
(502) 564-7140 *or*
(800) 626-2930

### Business Development

Business Information Clearinghouse
(502) 564-4252 *or*
(800) 626-2250 (in Kentucky)

Small and Minority Business Division
(502) 564-2064

Office of Business and Technology
(502) 564-4252

University of Kentucky's
Management Center
(606) 257-8746

### Financial Assistance

Commonwealth Small Business
Development Corp.
(502) 564-4320

Kentucky Agricultural Finance Corp.
(502) 564-2924

Kentucky Dept. of Financial Incentives
(502) 564-4554

Kentucky Investment Capital Network
(502) 564-7140

### Minority/Women's Opportunities

Small and Minority Business Division
(502) 564-2064

### Rural Development

Kentucky Rural Development
Authority
(502) 564-7670

### Small Business Development Centers

University of Kentucky
Center for Business Development
225 Business and Economics Bldg.
Lexington, KY 40506-0034
(606) 257-7668

Ashland; (606) 329-8011

Bowling Green; (502) 745-1905

Elizabethtown; (502) 765-6737

Highland Heights; (606) 572-6524

Hopkinsville; (502) 886-8666

Lexington; (606) 257-7666

Louisville (Bellarmine College);
(502) 452-8282

Louisville (University of Louisville);
(502) 852-7854

Middlesboro; (606) 242-2145, ext. 2034

Morehead; (606) 783-2895

Murray; (502) 762-2856

Owensboro; (502) 926-8085

Pikeville; (606) 432-5848

Somerset; (606) 677-6120

## Other Kentucky Resources

Kentucky Chamber of Commerce
464 Chenault Rd.
PO Box 817
Frankfurt, KY 40602
(502) 695-4700

Small Business Administration
District Office
600 Dr. M. L. King, Jr. Pl., Rm. 188
Louisville, KY 40202
(502) 582-5971

U.S. Dept. of Commerce District Office
601 W. Broadway, Rm. 634-B
Louisville, KY 40202-2243
(502) 582-5066

Internal Revenue Service
(800) 829-1040

## LOUISIANA

Dept. of Economic Development
PO Box 94185
Baton Rouge, LA 70804
(504) 342-3000
http://www.Idol.state.1a.us/ded/ded-
menu.htm

## Business Development

Office of Commerce and Industry,
Division of Business Services
(504) 342-5893

## Financial Assistance

Office of Commerce and Industry,
Financial Incentives
(504) 342-5398

Louisiana Economic Development Corp.
(504) 342-5675

## Minority/Women's Opportunities

Division of Minority and Women's
Business Enterprise
(504) 928-5373

## Small Business Development Centers

Northeast Louisiana University
College of Business
Administration, Rm. 2-57
Monroe, LA 71209-6435
(318) 342-5506

Alexandria; (318) 484-2123

Baton Rouge; (504) 922-0998

Hammond; (504) 549-3831

Lafayette; (318) 262-5344

Lake Charles; (318) 475-5529

Monroe; (318) 342-1224

Natchitoches; (318) 357-5611

New Orleans (Loyola University);
(504) 865-3474

New Orleans (Southern University);
(504) 286-5308

New Orleans (University of New Orleans);
(504) 539-9292

Ruston; (318) 257-3537

Shreveport; (318) 797-5144

Thibodaux; (504) 448-4242

## Other Louisiana Resources

Louisiana Association of Business
and Industry
PO Box 80258
Baton Rouge, LA 70898-0258
(504) 928-5388

Small Business Administration
District Office
4365 Canal St., Ste. 2250
New Orleans, LA 70130
(504) 589-2354

U.S. Dept. of Commerce District Office
One Canal Pl., Ste. 2150
New Orleans, LA 70130
(504) 589-6546

Internal Revenue Service
(800) 928-1040

## MAINE

Dept. of Economic and Community
Development
State House Station #59
Augusta, ME 04333-0949
(207) 287-2656

## Business Development

Office of Business Development
(207) 287-3153

Business Answers
(207) 287-3153 *or*

(800) 872-3838 (in Maine) *or*
(800) 541-5872 (outside Maine)

## Financial Assistance

Finance Authority of Maine
(207) 623-3263

Linked Investment Program
(207) 623-3263

## Small Business Development Centers

University of Southern Maine
93 Falmouth St.
PO Box 9300
Portland, ME 04104-9300
(207) 780-4420

Auburn; (207) 783-9186

Bangor; (207) 942-6389

Caribou; (207) 498-8736

Portland; (207) 780-4949

Sanford; (207) 324-0316

Wiscasset; (207) 882-4340

## Other Maine Resources

Maine Chamber of Commerce
and Industry
7 Community Dr.
Augusta, ME 04330-9412
(207) 623-4568

Small Business Administration
District Office
40 Western Ave., Rm. 512

Augusta, ME 04330
(207) 622-8378

U.S. Dept. of Commerce District Office
World Trade Center
Commonwealth Pier, Ste. 307
Boston, MA 02210
(617) 424-5950

Internal Revenue Service
(800) 829-1040

## MARYLAND

Dept. of Economic and Business
Development
Redwood Tower, 217 E. Redwood St.
Baltimore, MD 21202
(410) 767-6300

### Business Development

Office of Regional Response
(410) 767-0523

At-Risk Business
(410) 767-6517

Small Business Development
Center Network
(410) 767-6552

### Financial Assistance

Maryland Small Business Development
Financing Authority
(410) 767-6359

### International Trade

Trade Finance Program
(410) 767-6388

### Minority/Women's Opportunities

Office of Minority Affairs
(410) 767-8232

Procurement Office
(410) 767-2215

### Small Business Development Centers

College Park (University of Maryland)
(301) 405-1000

Annapolis; (410) 224-4205

Baltimore; (410) 605-0990

Bel Air; (410) 893-3837

Columbia; (410) 313-6550

Cumberland; (301) 724-6716

Elkton; (410) 392-0597

Frederick; (301) 846-2683

Great Mills; (301) 863-6679

Hagerstown; (301) 797-0327

Landover; (301) 883-6491

McHenry; (301) 387-3080

Owings Mills; (410) 356-2888

Rockville; (301) 217-2345

Salisbury; (410) 546-4325

Towson; (410) 832-5866

Waldorf; (301) 934-7583

Westminster; (410) 857-8166

Wye Mills; (410) 827-5286

### Other Maryland Resources

Maryland Chamber of Commerce
60 West St., Ste. 100
Annapolis, MD 21401
(410) 269-0642

Small Business Administration
District Office
10 S. Howard St., Rm. 6220
Baltimore, MD 21202
(410) 962-4392

U.S. Dept. of Commerce District Office
301 E. Pratt St., Ste. 2432
Baltimore, MD 21202-2525

Internal Revenue Service:
Baltimore; (410) 962-2590
Elsewhere; (800) 829-1040

### MASSACHUSETTS

Office of Business Development
One Ashburton Pl., Rm. 2101
Boston, MA 02108
(617) 727-3206

### Business Development

Massachusetts Business
Development Corp.
(617) 350-8877

Massachusetts Technology
Development Corp.
(617) 723-4920

### Financial Assistance

Massachusetts Industrial Finance
Authority
(617) 451-2477

Capital Formation Service
(617) 552-4091

Technology Capital Network, Inc.
(617) 253-7163

### International Trade

Office of International Trade and
Investment
(617) 367-1830

### Minority/Women's Opportunities

Office of Minority and Women's Business
Assistance
(617) 727-8692

### Small Business Development Centers

University of Massachusetts
Rm. 205, School of Management
Amherst, MA 01003
(413) 545-6301

Boston (NTC); (617) 478-4133

Boston (Minority Business Assistance
Center); (617) 287-7750

Chestnut Hill; (617) 552-4091

Fall River; (508) 673-9783

Salem; (508) 741-6343

Springfield; (413) 767-6712

Worcester; (508) 793-7615

**Other Massachusetts Resources**

West Suburban Chamber of Commerce
One Moody St., Ste. 301
Waltham, MA 02154
(617) 894-4700

Small Business Administration
District Offices
10 Causeway St., Rm. 265
Boston, MA 02222-1093
(617) 565-5590

Springfield Branch Office
1550 Main St., Rm. 212
Boston, MA 01103
(413) 785-0268

U.S. Dept. of Commerce District Office
World Trade Center
Commonwealth Pier, Ste. 307
Boston, MA 02210
(617) 424-5950

Internal Revenue Service
Boston; (617) 536-1040
Elsewhere; (800) 829-1040

## MICHIGAN

Michigan Jobs Commission
Victor Office Center, 4th Fl.
201 N. Washington Sq.
Lansing, MI 48913
(517) 373-9808

**Business Development**

Business Start-up Assistance
(517) 373-9808

Legal Assistance Referral Service
(517) 373-9808

Technology Consulting Referral Services
(517) 373-9808

Total Quality Management Assistance
(517) 373-9808

Economic/Labor Market Information
(517) 373-9808

Industry/Market Information
(517) 373-9808

Permitting Coordination
(517) 373-9808

Regulatory/Government Ombudsman
Service
(517) 373-9808

**Financial Assistance**

Business Operating Cost Estimating
Service
(517) 373-9808

Joint Venture Assistance
(517) 373-9808

Local Development Agencies
Coordination
(517) 373-9808

Tax Abatement Services
(517) 373-9808

Private Financing Referral Service
(517) 373-9808

Public Financing Program
(517) 373-9808

**Minority/Women's Opportunities**

Minority and Women-Owned
Business Services
(517) 373-9808

**Small Business Development Centers**

Wayne State University
2727 Second Ave., Rm. 107
Detroit, MI 48201
(313) 964-1798

Allendale; (616) 892-4120

Ann Arbor; (313) 930-0033

Bad Axe; (517) 269-6431

Benton Harbor; (616) 927-8179 *or*
(800) 252-1562

Big Rapids; (616) 592-3553

Brighton; (810) 227-3556

Cadillac; (616) 775-9776

Caro; (517) 673-2849

Detroit (Southeast Michigan Business
Assistance Consortium);
(313) 577-2788

Detroit (University of Detroit);
(313) 993-1115

Escanaba; (906) 786-9234

Flint; (810) 239-5847

Grand Haven; (616) 846-3153

Grand Rapids; (616) 771-6693

Hart; (616) 873-7141

Howell; (517) 546-4020

Kalamazoo; (616) 337-7350

Lansing; (517) 483-1921

Lapeer; (810) 667-0080

Marquette; (906) 228-5571

Mt. Clemens; (810) 469-5118

Mt. Pleasant; (517) 774-3270

Muskegon; (616) 722-3751

Port Huron; (810) 982-9511

Saline; (313) 944-1016

Scottville; (616) 845-6211, ext. 3104

Sidney; (517) 328-2111, ext. 354

Traverse City; (616) 922-1719

Traverse City (EDC); (616) 946-1596

Troy; (810) 952-5800

University Center; (517) 790-4388

Warren; (810) 751-3939

## Other Michigan Resources

Michigan Chamber of Commerce
600 S. Walnut St.
Lansing, MI 48933
(517) 371-2100

Small Business Administration
District Offices
477 Michigan Ave., Rm. 515
Detroit, MI 48226
(313) 226-6075

228 W. Washington, Ste. 11
Marquette, MI 49885
(906) 225-1108

U.S. Dept. of Commerce District Offices
477 Michigan Ave., Rm. 1140
Detroit, MI 48226-2518
(313) 226-3650

300 Monroe St. NW, Rm. 406-A
Grand Rapids, MI 49503
(616) 458-3564

Internal Revenue Service
Detroit; (313) 237-0800
Elsewhere; (800) 829-1040

## MINNESOTA

Small Business Assistance Office
500 Metro Sq., 121 Seventh Pl.
St. Paul, MN 55101-2146
(800) 657-3858

## Business Development

Bureau of Business Licenses
(612) 296-5023

Bureau of Small Business
(612) 296-3871

Small Business Development Center
(612) 297-5770

## Financial Assistance

Dept. of Trade and Economic
Development
(612) 297-1391

## International Trade

Minnesota Trade Office
(612) 297-4222

## Publication

*Joint Ventures*
Small Business Assistance Office
(612) 296-3871

## Small Business Development Centers

Dept. of Trade and Economic
Development
500 Metro Sq., 121 Seventh Pl. E
St. Paul, MN 55101-2146
(612) 297-5770

Bemidji; (218) 755-4286

Bloomington; (612) 832-6221

Brainerd; (218) 828-2525

Duluth; (218) 726-6192

Grand Rapids; (218) 327-2241

Hibbing; (218) 262-6703

International Falls; (218) 285-2255

Mankato; (507) 389-8863

Marshall; (507) 537-7386

Minneapolis; (612) 338-3280

Minneapolis (University of St. Thomas);
(612) 962-4500

Moorhead; (218) 236-2289

Owatonna; (507) 451-0517

Pine City; (612) 629-7340

Plymouth; (612) 550-7218

Red Wing; (612) 385-2243

Rochester; (507) 285-7536

Rosemount; (612) 423-8262

Rushford; (507) 864-7557

St. Cloud; (320) 255-4842

Virginia; (218) 741-4251

White Bear Lake; (612) 779-5764

### Other Minnesota Resources

Minnesota Chamber of Commerce
30 E. Seventh St., Ste. 1700
St. Paul, MN 55101
(612) 292-4650

Small Business Administration
District Office
100 N. Sixth St., Ste. 610-C
Minneapolis, MN 55403-1563
(612) 370-2324

U.S. Dept. of Commerce District Office
110 S. Fourth St., Rm. 108
Minneapolis, MN 55401-2227
(612) 348-1638

Internal Revenue Service
(800) 829-1040

### MISSISSIPPI

Mississippi Dept. of Economic and
Community Development
PO Box 849
Jackson, MS 39205-0849
(601) 359-3449
http://www.decd.state.ms.us

### Business Development

Business Incubator, Existing Business
and Industry
(601) 352-0957

Assistance Division
(601) 359-3593

Mississippi Enterprise for Technology
(601) 688-3144

### Financial Assistance

Mississippi Business Finance Corp.
(601) 359-3552

## Minority/Women's Opportunities

Jackson Minority Business
Development Center
(601) 362-2260

Minority Business Enterprise
(601) 359-3448

## Rural Development

Rural Economic Development Program
(601) 359-3552

## Small Business Development Centers

University of Mississippi
Old Chemistry Bldg., Ste. 216
University, MS 38677
(601) 232-5001

Booneville; (601) 728-7751

Cleveland; (601) 846-4236

Decatur; (601) 635-2111, ext. 297

Ellisville; (601) 477-4165

Gautier; (601) 497-7723

Greenville; (601) 378-8183

Gulfport; (601) 396-1288

Hattiesburg; (601) 544-0030

Itta Bena; (601) 254-3601

Jackson; (601) 968-2795

Long Beach; (601) 865-4578

Lorman; (601) 877-6684, ext. 3901

Meridian; (601) 482-7445

Mississippi State; (601) 325-8684

Natchez; (601) 445-5254

Raymond; (601) 857-3536

Ridgeland; (601) 853-0827

Southaven; (601) 342-7648

Summit; (601) 276-3890

Tupelo; (601) 680-8515

## Other Mississippi Resources

Mississippi Economic Council
620 North St., PO Box 23276
Jackson, MS 39225-3276
(601) 969-0022

Small Business Administration
District Offices
One Hancock Plaza, Ste. 1001
Gulfport, MS 39501-7758
(601) 863-4449
101 W. Capitol St., Ste. 400
Jackson, MS 39201
(601) 965-4378

U.S. Dept. of Commerce District Office
201 W. Capitol St., Ste. 310
Jackson, MS 39201-2005
(601) 965-4388

Internal Revenue Service
(800) 829-1040

## MISSOURI

Missouri Dept. of Economic Development
Truman State Office Bldg.
301 W. High St.
PO Box 1157
Jefferson City, MO 65102
(573) 751-4962
http://www.ecodev.state.mo.us/

### Business Development

Business Development Section
(573) 751-9045

Business Information Programs:
Missouri Business Assistance Center,
Missouri Economic Development Information System, Missouri Product Finder,
(573) 751-4982

Missouri Customized Training Program
(800) 877-8698

### Financial Assistance

Community and Economic Development
Finance Program
(573) 751-0717

### Minority/Women's Opportunities

Office of Minority Business
(573) 751-3237

Women's Council
 (573) 751-0810

### Rural Development

Agricultural and Small Business
Development Authority
(573) 751-2129

Office of Rural Development
(573) 751-1208

### Small Business Development Centers

University of Missouri
300 University Pl.
Columbia, MO 65211
(314) 882-7096

Cape Girardeau; (573) 290-5965

Chillicothe; (816) 646-6920

Joplin; (417) 625-9313

Kansas City; (816) 501-4572

Kirksville; (816) 785-4307

Maryville; (816) 562-1701

Mark Hills; (314) 431-4593, ext. 266

Rolla; (573) 341-4559

St. Louis; (314) 977-7232

Springfield; (417) 836-5685

Warrensburg; (816) 543-4402

### Other Missouri Resources

Missouri Chamber of Commerce
PO Box 149
Jefferson City, MO 65102
(573) 634-3511

Small Business Administration
District Offices
Lucas Pl., 323 W. Eighth St., Ste. 501

Kansas City, MO 64105
(816) 374-6708
815 Olive St., Rm. 242
St. Louis, MO 63101
(314) 539-6600

620 S. Glenstone St., Ste. 110
Springfield, MO 65802-3200
(417) 864-7670

U.S. Dept. of Commerce District Offices
6011 E. 12th St., Rm. 635
Kansas City, MO 64106-2808
(816) 426-3141

8182 Maryland Ave., Ste. 303
St. Louis, MO 63105-3786
(314) 425-3302

Internal Revenue Service
St. Louis; (314) 342-1040
Elsewhere; (800) 829-1040

## MONTANA

Dept. of Commerce
1424 Ninth Ave.
Helena, MT 59620-0501
(406) 444-3494

### Business Development

Economic Development Division
(406) 444-3814

Business Recruitment Program
(406) 444-4187

Census and Economic Information
Center
(406) 444-2896

Business Licensing Office
(406) 444-4109

### Financial Assistance

Microbusiness Finance Program
(406) 444-4187

Board of Investments
(406) 444-0001

CDBG Economic Development Program
(406) 444-2787

### Minority/Women's Opportunities

Disadvantaged Business and Women's
Business Procurement Assistance
(406) 444-6337

### Rural Development

Agriculture Development Council
(406) 444-2402

Dept. of Agriculture Marketing Program
(406) 444-2402

### Small Business Development Centers

Montana Dept. of Commerce
1424 Ninth Ave.
Helena, MT 59620
(406) 444-4780

Billings; (406) 256-6875

Bozeman; (406) 587-3113

Butte; (406) 782-7333

Havre; (406) 265-9226

Kalispell; (406) 758-5412

Missoula; (406) 728-9234

Sidney; (406) 482-5024

## Other Montana Resources

Montana Chamber of Commerce
2030 11th Ave.
PO Box 1730
Helena, MT 59624
(406) 444-3494

Small Business Administration
District Office
301 South Park
Drawer 10054, Rm. 334
Helena, MT 59626
(406) 441-1031

U.S. Dept. of Commerce District Office
1625 Broadway, Ste. 680
Denver, CO 80202-4706
(303) 844-6622

Internal Revenue Service
(800) 829-1040

## NEBRASKA

Nebraska Dept. of Economic
Development
PO Box 94666
301 Centennial Mall S
Lincoln, NE 68509-4666
(402) 471-3111

### Business Development

Existing Business Assistance Division
(402) 471-4167

One-Stop Business Assistance Center
(402) 471-3782

Industrial Training Programs
(402) 471-3780

Nebraska Business Development Center
(402) 595-2381

Nebraska's Ombudsman
(402) 471-2035

Entrepreneurship Projects
(402) 471-4803

Skill Training Employment Program
(402) 471-3780

### Financial Assistance

Export Promotion
(402) 471-4668

Nebraska Investment Finance Authority
(402) 434-3900

### Minority/Women's Opportunities

Office of Women's Business Ownership
(402) 221-3622

### Rural Development

Community and Rural Development
Division
(402) 471-3119

### Small Business Development Centers

University of Nebraska at Omaha
College of Business Administration Bldg.,
50th & Dodge St., Rm. 407
Omaha, NE 68182
(402) 554-2521

Chadron; (308) 432-6286

Kearney; (308) 865-8344

Lincoln; (402) 472-3358

North Platte; (308) 534-5115

Omaha; (402) 595-3511

Omaha (University of Nebraska); (402) 595-1281

Peru; (402) 872-2274

Scottsbluff; (308) 635-7513

Wayne; (402) 375-7575

## Other Nebraska Resources

Nebraska Chamber of Commerce
and Industry
1320 Lincoln Mall
PO Box 95128
Lincoln, NE 68509
(402) 474-4422

Small Business Administration
District Office
11141 Mill Valley Rd.
Omaha, NE 68154
(402) 221-3622

U.S. Dept. of Commerce
District Office
11135 O St.
Omaha, NE 68137-2337
(402) 221-3664

Internal Revenue Service
(800) 829-1040

## NEVADA

Nevada State Development Corp.
350 S. Center St., Ste. 310
Reno, NV 89501
(702) 323-3625

## Business Development

Nevada Dept. of Business and Industry
(702) 486-2750

Nevada State Development Corp.
(702) 323-3625

Nevada Self-Employment Trust
(702) 329-6789

## Financial Assistance

Department of Business and Industry
(702) 687-4250

Southern Nevada Certified
Development Co.
(702) 732-3998

Nevada Revolving Loan Fund Program
(702) 882-3882 *or*
(702) 687-1812

Nevada Commission on Economic
Development
(702) 687-4325

Nevada Development Capital Corp.
(702) 323-3625

Rural Nevada Development Corp.
(702) 289-8519

**Minority/Women's Opportunities**

Nevada Dept. of Business and Industry
(702) 486-2750

**Rural Development**

Nevada Commission on Economic
Development
(702) 687-4325

Rural Economic and Community
Development Service
(702) 887-1222

Rural Nevada Development Corp.
(702) 289-8519

**Small Business Development Centers**

University of Nevada at Reno
College of Business Administration
Mail Stop 032, 1664 N. Virginia St.
Reno, NV 89503
(702) 784-1717

Carson City; (702) 882-1565

Elko; (702) 753-2245

Incline Village; (702) 831-4440

Las Vegas; (702) 895-0852

North Las Vegas; (702) 399-6300

Winnemucca; (702) 623-5777

**Other Nevada Resources**

Nevada State Chamber of Commerce

405 Marsh Ave., PO Box 3499
Reno, NV 89505
(702) 686-3030

Small Business Administration
District Office
301 E. Stewart St., Rm. 301
PO Box 7527
Las Vegas, NV 89125-2527
(702) 388-6611

U.S. Dept. of Commerce District Office
17555 E. Plumb La., Ste. 152
Reno, NV 89502-3680
(702) 388-6611

Internal Revenue Service
(800) 829-1040

## NEW HAMPSHIRE

**Business Finance Authority**

New Hampshire Industrial
Development Authority
Four Park St., Ste. 302
Concord, NH 03301
http://www.state.nh.us/BFA/bfa.htm
(603) 271-2391

**Business Development**

Business Visitation Program
(603) 271-2591

Corporate Division
(603) 271-3244

New Hampshire Job Training
Council, Inc.
(603) 271-9500

New Hampshire Business
Development Corp.
(603) 623-5500

Office of Business and Industrial
Development
(603) 271-2591

### Financial Assistance

Business Finance Authority
(603) 271-2391

Office of Business and Industrial
Development
(603) 271-2591

Technology Capital Network, Inc.
(617) 253-7163

### Small Business Development Centers

University of New Hampshire
108 McConnell Hall
Durham, NH 03824
(603) 862-2200

Dover; (603) 749-4264

Keene; (603) 358-2602

Littleton; (603) 444-1053

Manchester; (603) 624-2000

Nashua; (603) 886-1233

Plymouth; (603) 535-2526

Portsmouth; (603) 334-6074

### Other New Hampshire Resources

Business and Industry Association of New
Hampshire
122 N. Main St.
Concord, NH 03301
(603) 224-5388

Small Business Administration
District Office
132 N. Main St., Suite 202
PO Box 1258
Concord, NH 03302-1258
(603) 225-1400

U.S. Dept. of Commerce District Office
World Trade Center
Commonwealth Pier, Ste. 307
Boston, MA 02210
(617) 424-5950

Internal Revenue Service
(800) 829-1040

### NEW JERSEY

Dept. of Commerce and Economic
Development
20 W. State St., CN 835
Trenton, NJ 08625
(609) 282-2444

### Business Development

Prospect Marketing
(609) 292-0700

### Financial Assistance

New Jersey Economic Development
Authority
(609) 292-1800

Commercial Lending
(609) 292-0187

**Minority/Women's Opportunities**

Division of Development for Small
Businesses and Women's and Minority
Businesses
(609) 292-3860

Certification Program
(609) 984-9834

**Rural Development**

Division of Rural Resources
(609) 292-5511

**Small Business Development Centers**

Rutgers University
Graduate School of Management
University Hgts, 180 University Ave.
Newark, NJ 07102
(201) 648-5950

Atlantic City; (609) 345-5600

Camden; (609) 225-6221

Lincroft; (908) 842-8685

Paramus; (201) 447-7841

Trenton; (609) 586-4800, ext. 469

Union; (908) 527-2946

Washington; (908) 689-9620

**Other New Jersey Resources**

New Jersey State Chamber of Commerce
50 W. State St., Ste. 1310
Trenton, NJ 08608
(609) 989-7888

Small Business Administration
District Office
2 Gateway Center, 4th Fl.
Newark, NJ 07102
(201) 645-2434

U.S. Dept. of Commerce District Office
3131 Princeton Pike, Bldg. 6, Ste. 100
Trenton, NJ 08648-2201
(609) 989-2100

Internal Revenue Service
(800) 829-1040

## NEW MEXICO

Economic Development Dept.
PO Box 20003
Santa Fe, NM 85704-5003
(505) 827-0300

**Business Development**

New Mexico Small Business
Development Center
(505) 438-1362

**Financial Assistance**

Economic Development Division
(505) 827-0300

## Minority/Women's Opportunities

Governor's Commission on the Status
of Women
(505) 841-8920

## Small Business Development Centers

Santa Fe Community College
PO Box 4187, S. Richards Ave.
Santa Fe, NM 87502-4187
(505) 438-1262

Alamogordo; (505) 434-5272

Albuquerque; (505) 224-4246

Carlsbad; (505) 887-6562

Clovis; (505) 769-4136

Espanola; (505) 747-2236

Farmington; (505) 599-0528

Gallup; (505) 722-2220

Grants; (505) 287-8221

Hobbs; (505) 392-5549

Las Cruces; (505) 527-7606

Las Vegas; (505) 454-2595

Los Alamos; (505) 662-0001

Los Lunas; (505) 925-8980

Roswell; (505) 624-7133

Silver City; (505) 538-6320

South Valley; (505) 248-0132

Tucumcari; (505) 461-4413, ext. 140

## Other New Mexico Resources

Association of Commerce and Industry
of New Mexico
2309 Renard Pl. SE, Ste. 402
Albuquerque, NM 87106
(505) 842-0644

Small Business Administration
District Office
625 Silver Ave. SW, Ste. 322
Albuquerque, NM 87106
(505) 766-1870

U.S. Dept. of Commerce District Office
1100 St. Francis Dr.
Santa Fe, NM 87503
(505) 827-0350

Internal Revenue Service
(800) 829-1040

## NEW YORK

Empire State Development Division
for Small Business
One Commerce Plaza
Albany, NY 12245
(518) 473-0499

## Business Development

Business Assistance Hot Line
(800) 782-8369

Business Service Ombudsman
(518) 473-0499 *or*
(212) 803-2289

Division for Small Business
(518) 473-0499

New York State Small Business
Advisory Board
(518) 473-0499

Small Business Advocacy Program
(518) 473-0499 *or*
(212) 803-2200

Office of Regulatory Reform
Business Permits
(518) 486-3292

### Financial Assistance

Empire State Development Corp.
(212) 803-3100

### Minority/Women's Opportunities

Entrepreneurial Assistance Program
(212) 803-2410

Minority and Women's Business
Division
(212) 803-2410

Minority and Women's Certification
(212) 803-2410

### Small Business Development Centers

State University of New York (SUNY);
SUNY Plaza S-523
Albany, NY 12246
(518) 443-5398 *or*
(800) 732-SBDC

Albany; (518) 442-5577

Binghamton; (607) 777-4024

Brockport; (716) 637-6660

Bronx; (718) 563-3570

Brooklyn; (718) 368-4619

Buffalo; (716) 878-4030

Corning; (607) 962-9461

Dobbs Ferry; (914) 674-7485

Farmingdale; (516) 420-2765

Fishkill; (914) 897-2607

Geneseo; (716) 245-5429

Jamaica; (718) 262-2880

Jamestown; (716) 665-5754

Kingston; (914) 339-0025

New York City; (212) 346-1900

Niagara Falls; (716) 285-4793

Oswego; (315) 343-1545

Plattsburgh; (518) 562-4260

Rochester; (716) 232-7310

Sanborn; (716) 693-1910

Southampton; (516) 287-0059

Staten Island; (718) 982-2560

Stony Brook; (516) 632-9070

Suffern; (914) 356-0370

Syracuse; (315) 492-3029

Utica; (315) 792-7546

Watertown; (315) 782-9292

White Plains; (914) 644-4116

## Other New York Resources

Business Council of New York State
152 Washington Ave.
Albany, NY 12210
(518) 465-7511

Small Business Administration
District Offices
111 W. Huron St., Rm. 1311
Buffalo, NY 14202
(716) 551-4301

333 E. Water St., 4th Fl.
Elmira, NY 14901
(607) 734-8130

35 Pinelawn Rd., Ste. 207W
Melville, NY 11747
(516) 454-0750

26 Federal Plaza, Rm. 3100
New York, NY 10278
(212) 264-4355

100 State St., Ste. 410
Rochester, NY 14614
(716) 263-6700

100 S. Clinton St., Rm. 1073
Syracuse, NY 13261
(315) 448-0423

U.S. Dept. of Commerce District Offices
Federal Bldg.
111 W. Huron St., Rm. 1304
Buffalo, NY 14202-2301
(716) 551-4191

6 World Trade Center, Rm. 635
New York, NY 10048
(212) 264-0635

111 East Ave, Ste. 220
Rochester, NY 14604-2520
(716) 263-6480

Internal Revenue Service
Buffalo; (716) 685-5432
Elsewhere; (800) 829-1040

## NORTH CAROLINA

Small Business and Technology
Development Center
Fayetteville Street Mall
Raleigh, NC 27603
(919) 715-7272, ext.333
http://www.commerce.state.nc.us

## Business Development

Business License Information Office
(919) 733-0641

Small Business and Technology
Development Center
(919) 715-7272

## Financial Assistance

Small Business and Technology
Development Center
(919) 715-7272

## Rural Development

Rural Economic Development Center
(919) 715-2725

## Small Business Development Centers

University of North Carolina
333 Fayette Street Mall, Ste. 1150
Raleigh, NC 27601-1742
(919) 715-7272 *or*
(800) 258-0862

Asheville; (704) 251-6025

Boone; (704) 262-2492

Chapel Hill; (919) 962-0389

Charlotte; (704) 548-1090

Cullowhee; (704) 227-3247

Elizabeth City; (919) 335-3247

Fayetteville; (910) 486-1727

Greensboro; (910) 334-7005

Greenville; (919) 328-6183

Hickory; (704) 345-1110

Pembroke; (910) 521-6603

Rocky Mount; (919) 985-5130

Wilmington; (910) 395-3744

Winston-Salem; (910) 750-2030

## Other North Carolina Resources

North Carolina Citizens for Business
and Industry
225 Hillsborough St., Ste. 460
PO Box 2508
Raleigh, NC 27602
(919) 836-1400

Small Business Administration
District Office
200 N. College St., Ste. A2015
Charlotte, NC 28202-2137
(704) 344-6563

U.S. Dept. of Commerce District Office
400 W. Market St., Ste. 400
Greensboro, NC 27401-2241
(910) 333-5345

Internal Revenue Service
(800) 829-1040

# NORTH DAKOTA

Dept. of Economic Development
and Finance
1833 E. Bismarck Expy.
Bismarck, ND 58504
(701) 328-5300

## Business Development

Agricultural Product Utilization Grant
(701) 328-4760

Business and Community Assistance
Center, Minot State University
(701) 858-3825

Institute for Business and Industry
Development
(701) 231-1001

Center for Innovation and Business
Development
(701) 777-3132

**Financial Assistance**

Economic Development and Finance
(701) 328-5300

**International Trade**

Economic Development and Finance
(701) 328-5300

**Minority/Women's Opportunities**

Native American Business Assistance
(701) 328-5300

Women's Business Development
(701) 328-5300

**Rural Development**

Rural Economic and Community
Development
(701) 250-4791

**Small Business Development Centers**

University of North Dakota
118 Gamble Hall
Grand Forks, ND 58202-7308
(701) 777-3700 *or*
(800) 445-7232

Bismarck; (701) 223-8583

Dickinson; (701) 227-2096

Fargo; (701) 237-0986

Grand Forks; (701) 772-8502

Minot; (701) 852-886

**Other North Dakota Resources**

Greater North Dakota Association/
State Chamber of Commerce
2000 Schafer St.
PO Box 2639
Bismarck, ND 58502
(701) 222-0929

Small Business Association
District Office
657 Second Ave. N, Rm. 219
PO Box 3086
Fargo, ND 58108-3086
(701) 239-5131

U.S. Dept. of Commerce District Office
11135 O St.
Omaha, NE 68137-2337
(402) 221-3664

Internal Revenue Service
(800) 829-1040

**OHIO**

Office of Small Business
Ohio Dept. of Development
77 S. High St.
PO Box 1001
Columbus, OH 43216-1001
(614) 466-2718

## Business Development

One-Stop Business Permit Center
(614) 466-4232

## Financial Assistance

Office of Minority Financial Incentives
(614) 644-7708

Business Loans
(614) 466-5420

## Minority/Women's Opportunities

Women's Business Resource Program
(614) 466-4945

Minority Business
Development Program
(614) 466-5700

## Small Business Development Centers

Ohio Dept. of Development
77 S. High St.
PO Box 1001
Columbus, OH 43226-1001
(614) 466-2711

Akron; (330) 379-3170

Athens; (614) 572-1188

Athens (Ohio University);
(614) 593-1797

Bowling Green; (419) 352-3817

Canton; (330) 499-9600, ext. 683

Celina; (419) 586-0355

Cincinnati; (513) 948-2082

Cincinnati (COC); (513) 753-7141

Cleveland; (216) 621-3300, ext. 219

Cleveland; (216) 432-5364

Columbus; (614) 225-6910

Columbus (COC); (614) 225-6081

Coshocton; (614) 622-5435

Dayton; (513) 873-3503

Dayton (COC); (513) 226-8230

Defiance; (419) 784-3777

Fremont; (419) 332-1002 ext. 210

Jefferson (EDC); (216) 576-9134

Kettering; (513) 259-1361

Kirtland; (216) 951-1290

Lima; (519) 229-5320

Lorain; (216) 233-6500

Marietta; (614) 376-4832

Marion; (614) 387-0188

Middletown; (513) 422-4551

New Philadelphia; (330) 339-9070

Piketon; (614) 289-3727

Piqua; (513) 778-8419

Portsmouth; (614) 355-2316

Salem; (330) 332-0361, ext. 221

Southpoint; (614) 894-3838

Springfield; (513) 322-7821

St. Clairsville; (614) 695-9678

Steubenville; (614) 282-6226

Toledo; (419) 243-8191, ext. 224

Youngstown; (330) 746-3350

Zanesville; (614) 452-4868

**Other Ohio Resources**

Ohio Chamber of Commerce
230 E. Town St., PO Box 15159
Columbus, OH 43215-0154
(614) 228-4201

Small Business Administration
District Offices
525 Vine St., Ste. 870
Cincinnati, OH 45202
(513) 684-2814

1111 Superior Ave., Ste. 630
Cleveland, OH 44114-2507
(216) 522-4750

2 Nationwide Plaza, Ste. 1400
Columbus, OH 43215-2542
(614) 469-6860

U.S. Dept. of Commerce District Offices
Federal Office Bldg.
550 Main St., Rm. 9504
Cincinnati, OH 45202
(513) 684-2944

600 Superior Ave. E, Rm. 700
Cleveland, OH 44114-2650
(216) 522-4750

Internal Revenue Service
Cleveland; (216) 522-3000
Cincinnati; (513) 621-6281
Elsewhere; (800) 829-1040

## OKLAHOMA

Oklahoma Dept. of Commerce
6601 Broadway Ext., Bldg. 5
Oklahoma City, OK 73116
(405) 843-9770

**Business Development**

Business Development Division
(405) 841-5167

Main Street Program
(405) 841-5124

Business Service Program
(405) 841-5227

Training for Industry Program
(405) 841-5110

Research and Planning Division
(405) 841-5170

Community Affairs and
Development Division
(405) 841-9326

## Financial Assistance

Capital Resources Network
(405) 841-5140

Oklahoma Development Finance
Authority
(405) 848-9761

## Minority/Women's Opportunities

Minority Business Assistance
(405) 841-5227

Women-Owned Certification
(405) 841-5242

Tribal Government Assistance
(405) 841-5138

## Rural Development

Agricultural Linked Deposit Program
(405) 521-3191

Rural Development Office
(405) 843-9770, ext. 354

Rural Enterprises, Inc.
(405) 924-5094

## Small Business Development Centers

Southeastern State University
517 W. University
Durant, OK 74730
(405) 924-0277 *or*
(800) 522-6154

Ada; (405) 436-3190

Alva; (405) 327-8608

Enid; (405) 242-7989

Langston; (405) 466-3256

Lawton; (405) 248-4946

Miami; (918) 540-0575

Midwest City; (405) 733-7348

Oklahoma City; (405) 232-1968

Poteau; (918) 647-4019

Tahlequah; (918) 458-0802

Tulsa; (918) 581-2502

Weatherford; (405) 774-1040

## Other Oklahoma Resources

Oklahoma State Chamber of Commerce
and Industry
330 NE 10th St.
Oklahoma City, OK 73104
(405) 235-3669

Small Business Administration
District Office
210 W. Park Ave., Ste. 1300
Oklahoma City, OK 73116
(405) 231-5521

U.S. Dept. of Commerce District Offices
Oklahoma City
6601 Broadway Extension
Oklahoma City, OK 73116
(405) 231-5302

440 Houston St., Rm. 505
Tulsa, OK 74127-8913
(918) 581-7650

Internal Revenue Service
(800) 829-1040

## OREGON

Economic Development Office
775 Summer St. NE
Salem, OR 97310
(503) 986-0123

### Business Development

Marketing Services
(503) 986-0111

Business Information Center
(503) 986-2222

### Financial Assistance

Business Finance Section
(503) 986-0160

### Minority/Women's Opportunities

Oregon Dept. of Transportation
(503) 986-2643

Office of Minority, Women's, and
Emerging Small Businesses
(503) 378-5651

### Small Business Development Centers

Lane Community College
44 W. Broadway, Ste. 501
Eugene, OR 97401-3021
(541) 726-2250

Albany; (541) 917-4923

Ashland; (541) 722-3478

Bend; (541) 383-7290

Coos Bay; (541) 269-0123

Eugene; (541) 726-2255

Grants Pass; (541) 471-3515

Gresham; (503) 667-7658

Klamath Falls; (541) 885-1760

LaGrande; (541) 962-3391

Lincoln City; (541) 994-4166

Medford; (541) 772-3478

Milwaukie; (503) 656-4447

Ontario; (541) 889-2617

Pendleton; (541) 276-6233

Portland (CC); (503) 978-5080

Portland (ITP); (503) 274-7482

Roseburg; (541) 672-2535

Salem; (503) 399-5088

Seaside; (503) 738-3347

The Dalles; (541) 298-3118

Tillamook; (503) 942-2551

### Other Oregon Resources

Associated Oregon Industries, Inc.
1149 Court St. NE
PO Box 12519
Salem, OR 97309
(503) 588-0050

Small Business Administration
District Office
222 S.W. Columbia St., Ste. 500
Portland, OR 97201-6605
(503) 326-2682

U.S. Dept. of Commerce District Office
121 S.W. Salmon St., Ste. 242
Portland, OR 97204-2911
(503) 326-3001

Internal Revenue Service
Portland; (503) 221-3960
Elsewhere; (800) 829-1040

Oregon Department of Revenue, Tax Help
(503) 378-4988

## PENNSYLVANIA

Dept. of Commerce
Forum Bldg.
Harrisburg, PA 17120
(717) 783-8950

### Business Development

Small Business Resource Center
(717) 783-5700

Office of the Environmental Advocate
(717) 772-2889

Office of Entrepreneurial Assistance
(717) 783-8950

Office of Small Business Advocate
(717) 783-2525

### Financial Assistance

Air Quality Improvement Fund
(717) 787-9152

Employee Ownership Assistance Program
(717) 787-7120

Machine and Equipment Loan Fund
(717) 783-5046

Pennsylvania Capital Access Program
(717) 783-1109

Pennsylvania Capital Loan Fund
(717) 783-1768

Pennsylvania Economic Development
Financing Authority
(717) 783-1108

Pennsylvania Industrial Development
Authority
(717) 787-6245

Pennsylvania Minority Business
Development Authority
(717) 783-1127

Recycling Incentive Development
Account
(717) 783-5047

Revenue Bond and Mortgage Program
(717) 783-1108

Storage Tank Loan Fund
(717) 783-5047

## Minority/Women's Opportunities

Women's Business Advocate and
Entrepreneurial Assistance
(717) 787-3339

Governor's Advisory Commission on
African American Affairs
(717) 772-5085

Governor's Advisory Commission on
Latino Affairs
(717) 783-3877

Bureau of Contract Administration and
Business Development
(717) 787-7380

## Small Business Development Centers

University of Pennsylvania
The Wharton School
Vance Hall, 4th Fl.
3733 Spruce St.
Philadelphia, PA 19104-6374
(215) 898-1219

Bethlehem; (610) 758-3980

Clarion; (814) 226-2060

Erie; (814) 871-7714

Exton; (610) 436-2162

Harrisburg; (717) 720-4230

Indiana; (412) 357-7915

Latrobe; (412) 537-4572

Lewisburg; (717) 524-1249

Loretto; (814) 472-3200

Philadelphia (Temple University);
(215) 204-7282

Philadelphia (University of
Pennsylvania)
(215) 898-4861

Pittsburgh (Duquesne University);
(412) 396-6233

Pittsburgh (University of Pittsburgh);
(412) 648-1544

Scranton; (717) 941-7588

Wilkes-Barre; (717) 831-4340

## Other Pennsylvania Resources

Pennsylvania Chamber of Business
and Industry
One Commerce Sq.
417 Walnut St.
Harrisburg, PA 17101
(717) 255-3252

Small Business Administration
District Offices
100 Chestnut St., Rm. 309
Harrisburg, PA 17101
(717) 782-3840

475 Allendale Rd., St. 201
King of Prussia, PA 19406
(610) 962-3800

960 Penn Ave., 5th Fl.
Pittsburgh, PA 15222
(412) 644-2780

20 N. Pennsylvania Ave., Rm. 2327
Wilkes-Barre, PA 18701-3589
(717) 826-6497

U.S. Dept. of Commerce District Offices
615 Chestnut St., Ste. 1501
Philadelphia, PA 19106
(215) 597-6101

1000 Liberty Ave., Rm. 2002
Pittsburgh, PA 15222-4194
(412) 644-2850

Internal Revenue Service
Philadelphia; (215) 574-9900
Pittsburgh; (412) 281-0112
Elsewhere; (800) 829-1040

## PUERTO RICO

Dept. of Economic Development
and Commerce
PO Box 4435
San Juan, PR 00902-4435
(809) 721-2898

### Business Development

Office of Ombudsman
(809) 724-7373

Commercial Development Administration
(809) 721-3290

### Financial Assistance

Economic Development Bank
for Puerto Rico
(809) 766-4300

Economic Development Administration
(809) 758-4747

Government Bank for Puerto Rico
(809) 722-3760

### Small Business Development Centers

University of Puerto Rico at Mayaguez
Building B, 2nd Fl.
PO Box 5253, College Station
Mayaguez, PR 00681
(809) 834-3590

Humaca; (809) 850-2500

Ponce; (809) 841-2641

Rio Piedras; (809) 763-5880

San Juan; (809) 765-2335

### Other Puerto Rico Resources

Chamber of Commerce of Puerto Rico
100 Tetuan St.
Old San Juan, PR 00901
(809) 721-3290

Small Business Administration
District Office
Citibank Bldg.
252 Ponce de Leon Ave., Ste. 201
Hato Rey, PR 00918
(809) 766-5572

U.S. Dept. of Commerce District Office
Federal Bldg.
Room G-55, Chardon Ave.
Hato Rey, PR 00918
(809) 766-5555

## RHODE ISLAND

Rhode Island Economic
Development Corp.
1 W. Exchange St.
Providence, RI 02903
(401) 277-2601

### Business Development

Business Development Division
(401) 277-2601

### Financial Assistance

Financing Programs
(401) 277-2601, ext. 110

Small Business Loan Fund
(401) 277-2601, ext. 110

### Procurement Assistance

Federal Procurement Program
(401) 277-2601, ext. 147

### Small Business Development Centers

Bryant College Small Business
Development Center
1150 Douglas Pike
Smithfield, RI 02917-1282
(401) 232-6111

North Kingston; (401) 294-1228

Providence; (401) 831-1330

### Other Rhode Island Resources

Greater Providence Chamber of
Commerce
30 Exchange Terr.
Providence, RI 02903
(401) 821-5000

Small Business Administration
District Office
380 Westminster St.
Providence, RI 02903
(401) 528-4584

U.S. Dept. of Commerce District Office
1 W. Exchange St.
Providence, RI 02903
(401) 528-5104

Internal Revenue Service
(800) 829-1040

## SOUTH CAROLINA

Small and Minority Business Assistance
1205 Pendleton St.
Columbia, SC 29201
(803) 734-0657

### Business Development

Center for Applied Technology
(803) 646-4000

Existing Business and Industry
Services Dept.
(803) 737-4000

### Financial Assistance

Jobs Economic Development Authority
(803) 737-0079

### Minority/Women's Opportunities

Office of Small and Minority
Business Assistance
(803) 734-0657

## Rural Development

Dept. of Agriculture, Small Farms
Program
(803) 734-2210

## Small Business Development Centers

University of South Carolina
College of Business Administration
Columbia, SC 29208
(803) 777-4907

Aiken; (803) 641-3646

Beaufort; (803) 521-4143

Charleston; (803) 740-6160

Clemson; (864) 656-3227

Columbia; (803) 777-5118

Conway; (803) 349-2170

Florence; (803) 661-8256

Greenville; (864) 250-8894

Greenwood; (864) 941-8071

Orangeburg; (803) 536-8445

Rock Hill; (803) 323-2283

Spartanburg; (864) 594-5080

## Other South Carolina Resources

South Carolina Chamber of Commerce
1835 Assembly St., Ste. 172
Columbia, SC 29201-2440
(803) 765-4345

Internal Revenue Service
(800) 829-1040

## SOUTH DAKOTA

Governor's Office of Economic
Development
711 E. Wells Ave.
Pierre, SD 57501-3369
(605) 773-5032

## Business Development

Business Location Services
(605) 773-5032

Business Research Bureau
(605) 677-5287

## Financial Assistance

Financial Packaging
(605) 773-5032

Economic Development Finance
Authority
(605) 773-5032

Revolving Economic Development
and Initiative Fund
(605) 773-5032

## Rural Development

Agricultural Development Loan
Participation Program
(605) 773-5436

Participation Program
(605) 773-5436

Agricultural Processing
(605) 773-3375

Cooperative Extension Service
(605) 688-4147

## Small Business Development Centers

University of South Dakota
School of Business
Patterson Hall 115
414 E. Clarke St.
Vermillion, SD 57069
(605) 677-5498

Aberdeen; (605) 626-2565

Rapid City; (605) 394-5311

Sioux Falls; (605) 367-5753

## Other South Dakota Resources

Industry and Commerce Association
of South Dakota
108 N. Euclid Ave.
PO Box 190
Pierre, SD 57501
(605) 224-6161

Small Business Administration
District Office
110 S. Phillips, Ste. 200
Sioux Falls, SD 57102-1109
(605) 330-4231

U.S. Dept. of Commerce District Office
11135 O St.
Omaha, NE 68137-2337
(402) 221-3664

Internal Revenue Service
(800) 829-1040

## TENNESSEE

Dept. of Economic and Community
Development
320 Sixth Ave. N
Nashville, TN 37243
(800) 872-7201 (in Tennessee)
(800) 251-8594 (outside Tennessee)

## Business Development

Small Business Office
Center for Industrial Services
(615) 532-8657

SCORE; (615) 736-7621

## Minority/Women's Opportunities

Office of Minority Business Enterprise
(615) 741-2545

Women Business Owners
(615) 741-2545

Minority Business Development Center
(615) 255-0432

## Small Business Development Centers

University of Memphis
South Campus (Getwell Rd.), Bldg. #1
Memphis, TN
(901) 678-2500

Chattanooga; (423) 266-5781

Chattanooga (CC); (423) 752-1774

Clarksville; (615) 648-7764

Cleveland; (423) 478-6247

Columbia; (615) 388-5674

Dyersburg; (901) 286-3201

Hartsville; (615) 374-9521

Jackson (Jackson St. Community
College); (901) 424-5389

Jackson (Lambuth University);
(901) 425-3327

Johnson City; (423) 929-5630

Kingsport; (423) 392-8017

Knoxville; (423) 525-0277

Knoxville (ITC); (423) 637-4283

Memphis (ITC); (901) 678-4174

Memphis (University of Memphis);
(901) 527-1041

Morristown; (423) 585-2675

Murfreesboro; (615) 898-2745

Nashville; (615) 963-7179

## Other Tennessee Resources

Tennessee Association of Business
611 Commerce St., Ste. 3030

Nashville, TN 37203-3742
(615) 256-5141

Small Business Administration
District Office
50 Vantage Way, Ste. 201
Nashville, TN 37228-1500
(615) 736-5881

U.S. Dept. of Commerce District Offices
301 E. Church Ave.
Knoxville, TN 37915-2572
(423) 545-4637
22 N. Front St., Ste. 200, Falls Bldg.
Memphis, TN 38103-2190
(901) 544-4137

404 James Robertson Pkwy., #114
Nashville, TN 37219-1505
(615) 736-5161

Internal Revenue Service
Nashville; (615) 834-9005
Elsewhere; (800) 829-1040

## TEXAS

Texas Dept. of Commerce
1700 N. Congress Ave.
PO Box 12728
Austin, TX 78711
(512) 936-0100

**Business Development**

Texas-One; (512) 936-0237

Business Development Division
(512) 936-0223

Information and Research
(512) 936-0081

Business Information and Referral
(800) 888-0581

Office of Trade and International
Relations
(512) 936-0249

Job Training Partnership Act Program
(512) 936-0345

Growth-Retention
(512) 936-0254

Community Assistance/Small Business
(512) 936-0223

**Financial Assistance**

Business Services
(512) 936-0282

Capital Development
(512) 936-0260

Enterprise Zone
(512) 936-0270

Smart Jobs
(800) 888-0511 *or* (512) 936-0500

Texas Manufacturing Assistance Center
(512) 936-0235

**Minority/Women's Opportunities**

Community Assistance/Small Business
(512) 936-0223

**Rural Development**

Community Assistance/Small Business
(512) 936-0223

Association of Business and Chambers
of Commerce
1209 Nueces
Austin, TX 78701
(512) 472-1594

**Small Business Development Centers**

Dallas County Community College
North Texas Small Business Center
1402 Corinth St., Ste. 2111
Dallas, TX 75215
(214) 860-5831

Houston Small Business
Development Center
1100 Louisiana, Ste. 500
Houston, TX 77002
(713) 752-8400

Lubbock Small Business
Development Center
2579 S. Loop 289
Lubbock, TX 79423
(806) 745-3973

University of Texas, San Antonio
1222 N. Main
San Antonio, TX
(210) 558-2460

Abilene; (915) 670-0300

Alpine; (915) 837-8694

Alvin; (713) 388-4922

Amarillo; (806) 372-5151

Athens; (903) 675-7403

Austin; (512) 473-3510

Baytown; (713) 425-6309

Beaumont; (409) 880-2367

Brenham; (409) 830-4137

Bryan; (409) 260-5222

Corpus Christi; (512) 881-1888

Corsicana; (903) 874-0658

Dallas; (214) 860-5850

Dallas (ITC); (214) 747-1300

Dallas (Proc.); (214) 860-5842

Dallas (Technical Assistance);
(214) 860-5852

Denison; (903) 786-3551

Duncanville; (214) 709-5878

Edinburg; (210) 316-2610

El Paso; (915) 534-3410

Ft. Worth; (817) 794-5978

Gainesville; (817) 668-4220

Galveston; (409) 740-7380

Houston; (713) 591-9320

Houston (ITC); (713) 752-8404

Houston (Proc.); (713) 752-8477

Huntsville; (409) 294-3737

Kingsville; (512) 595-5088

Lake Jackson; (409) 266-3380

Laredo; (210) 722-0563

Longview; (903) 757-5857

Lubbock; (806) 745-1637

Lufkin; (409) 639-1887

Mt. Pleasant; (800) 357-7232

Odessa; (915) 552-2455

Paris; (903) 784-1802

Plano; (214) 985-3770

San Angelo; (915) 942-2098

San Antonio; (210) 558-2458

Stafford; (713) 933-7932

Stephenville; (817) 968-9330

Texas City; (409) 938-7578

Tyler; (903) 510-2975

Uvalde; (210) 278-2527

Victoria; (512) 575-8944

Waco; (817) 714-0077

Wichita Falls; (817) 689-4373

**Other Texas Resources**

Small Business Association District Offices
606 N. Carancabua, Ste. 1200
Corpus Christi, TX 78476
(512) 888-3333

10737 Gateway W., Ste. 320
El Paso, TX 799353
(915) 540-5155

4300 Amon Carter Blvd., Ste. 114,
Ft. Worth, TX 76155
(817) 885-6500

222 E. Van Buren St., Rm. 500
Harlingen, TX 7855-6855
(210) 427-5625

9301 S.W. Freeway, Ste. 550
Houston, TX 77074-1591
(713) 773-6500

1611 Tenth St., Ste. 200
Lubbock, TX 79401-2693
(806) 743-7462

727 E. Durango Blvd., Ste. A-527
San Antonio, TX 78206-1204
(210) 472-5900

U.S. Dept. of Commerce District Offices
410 E. 5th St., 4th Fl.
Anson Jones Bldg.
Austin TX 78701-3706
(512) 936-0442

2050 N. Stemmons Fwy., Ste. 170
Dallas, TX 75207
(214) 767-0543

500 Dallas St., 1 Allen Center, Ste. 1160
Houston, TX 77002-4802
(713) 718-3062

Internal Revenue Service
Dallas; (214) 742-2440
Houston; (713) 541-0440
Elsewhere; (800) 829-1040

## UTAH

Community and Economic
Development
24 S. State St., Ste. 500
Salt Lake City, UT 84111
(801) 538-8700

**Business Development**

Business Expansion and Retention
(801) 538-8775

Small Business Development Center
(801) 255-5991

**Financial Assistance**

Economic Development Corp. of Utah
(801) 328-8824

Utah Capital Access Act
(801) 538-8776

Utah Microenterprise Loan Fund
(801) 269-8408

Utah Technology Finance Corp.
(801) 364-4346

## Minority Opportunities

Office of Asian Affairs
(801) 538-8883

Office of Black Affairs
(801) 538-8829

Office of Hispanic Affairs
(801) 538-8850

Office of Indian Affairs
(801) 538-8808

Office of Polynesian Affairs
(801) 538-8691

## Rural Development

Rural Business Development
(801) 538-8781

## Small Business Development Centers

University of Utah
8811 S. 700 East
Sandy, UT 84070
(801) 255-5991

Cedar City; (801) 586-5400

Ephraim; (801) 283-4021, ext. 207

Logan; (801) 797-2277

Ogden; (801) 626-7232

Orem; (801) 222-8230

Price; (801) 637-5032

Roosevelt; (801) 722-4523

St. George; (801) 652-7732

## Other Utah Resources

Utah State Chamber of Commerce
Association
c/o Sugar House Area Chamber
of Commerce
1095 E. 2100 South
Salt Lake City, UT 8413
(801) 467-0844

Small Business Administration
District Office
125 S. State St., Rm. 2237
Salt Lake City, UT 84138-1195
(801) 524-3209

U.S. Dept. of Commerce District Office
324 S. State St., Ste. 105
Salt Lake City, UT 84111-8321
(801) 524-5116

Internal Revenue Service
(800) 829-1040

## VERMONT

Vermont Dept. of Economic
Development
109 State St.
Montpelier, VT 05602
(802) 828-3221

**Business Development**

Ombudsman Permit Program
(802) 828-3221

Small Business Development Center
(802) 728-9101

**Financial Assistance**

Vermont Council on Rural Development
(802) 775-0871

Vermont Economic Development
Authority
(802) 223-7226

Vermont Job Start
(802) 229-5627

**Minority/Women's Opportunities**

Government Assistance Program
(802) 828-3221

**Rural Development**

Vermont Council on Rural Development
(802) 775-0871

**Small Business Development Centers**

Vermont Technical College
(802) 728-9101 *or*
(800) 464-SBDC

Brattleboro; (802) 275-7731

Burlington; (802) 658-9228

Middlebury; (802) 388-7953

Montpelier; (802) 223-4654

North Bennington; (802) 442-8975

Rutland; (802) 773-9147

Springfield; (802) 885-2071

St. Johnsbury; (802) 748-1014

**Other Vermont Resources**

Vermont Chamber of Commerce
PO Box 37
Montpelier, VT 05601
(802) 223-3443

Small Business Administration
District Office
87 State St., Rm. 205
PO Box 605
Montpelier, VT 05601
(802) 828-4422

U.S. Dept. of Commerce District Office
World Trade Center
Commonwealth Pier, Ste. 307
Boston, MA 02210-2075
(617) 424-5950

Internal Revenue Service
(800) 829-1040

### VIRGINIA

Virginia Small Business Development
Network
Virginia Dept. of Economic Development
PO Box 798
Richmond, VA 23206-0798
(804) 371-8253

## Business Development

Small Business Development Center
(804) 371-8253

Dept. of Professional and Occupational
Regulation Licensing
(804) 367-8500

## Financial Assistance

Virginia Small Business Financing
Authority
(804) 371-8254

## International Trade

Export Financing Program
(804) 371-8255

## Minority/Women's Opportunities

Dept. of Minority Business Enterprise
(804) 786-5560

Virginia Dept. of Transportation
(804) 786-2085

## Publication

*Virginia Capital Resource Directory*
(804) 371-8254

## Small Business Development Centers

Commonwealth of Virginia
Dept. of Economic Development
(804) 371-8253

Virginia Business Development Network
901 E. Byrd St., W. Tower, 19th Fl.
Richmond, VA 23206

Abingdon; (540) 676-5615

Arlington; (703) 993-8128

Big Stone Gap; (540) 523-6529

Blacksburg; (540) 231-4004

Blacksburg (Virginia Polytechnic Institute
and State University);
(540) 231-5278

Charlottesville; (804) 295-8198

Fairfax; (703) 277-7700

Farmville; (804) 395-2086

Fredericksburg; (540) 654-1060

Hampton; (757) 825-2957

Harrisonburg; (540) 568-3227

Lynchburg; (804) 582-6170

Manassas; (703) 335-2500

Middletown; (540) 869-6649

Norfolk; (757) 622-6414

Richlands; (540) 964-7345

Richmond; (800) 646-7232

Roanoke; (540) 983-0717

South Boston; (804) 575-0044

Sterling; (703) 430-7222

Warsaw; (804) 333-0286

Wytheville; (540) 223-4798

## Other Virginia Resources

The Virginia Chamber of Commerce
9 S. Fifth St.
Richmond, VA 23219
(804) 644-1607

Small Business Administration
District Office
1504 Santa Rosa Rd., Ste. 200
Richmond, VA 23229
(804) 771-2400

U.S. Dept. of Commerce District Office
700 Center, 704 E Franklin St., Ste. 550
Richmond, VA 23219
(804) 771-2246

Internal Revenue Service
Richmond; (804) 698-5000
Elsewhere; (800) 829-1040

## WASHINGTON

Business Assistance Center
Dept. of Community, Trade
and Economic Development
906 Columbia St. SW
PO Box 48300
Olympia, WA 98504-8300
(360) 753-4900

## Business Development

Business Development
(206) 464-7255

Business License Service
(360) 753-4401

Innovation and Technology Development
Assistance Program
(206) 464-5450

Small Business Development Center
(509) 335-1576

Small Business Ombudsman
(360) 586-3022

Small Business Hotline
(360) 664-9501 *or*
(800) 237-1233 (in Washington)

## Financial Assistance

Community Development Finance
Program
(360) 753-4900

Development Loan Fund
(360) 753-4900

Small Business Finance Unit
(360) 753-4900

Washington Economic Development
Finance Authority
(206) 389-2559

## Minority/Women's Opportunities

Minority and Women's Business
Development
(206) 389-2561

**Rural Development**

Dept. of Community, Trade and
Economic Development
(360) 586-8979

**Publication**

*Financing a Business*
(360) 664-9501 *or*
(800) 237-1233 (in Washington)

**Small Business Development Centers**

Washington State University
Johnson Tower 501
Pullman, WA 99164-4851
(509) 335-1576

Aberdeen; (360) 538-4021

Bellevue; (206) 643-2888

Bellingham; (360) 650-3899

Centralia; (360) 736-9391, x483

Kenliewick; (509) 735-6222

Lynwood; (206) 640-1435

Moses Lake; (509) 762-6289

Mt. Vernon; (360) 416-7872

Okanogan; (509) 826-5107

Olympia; (360) 753-5616

Port Angeles; (360) 457-7793

Seattle; (206) 464-5450

Seattle; (Duwamish Industrial
Education Center); (206) 764-5475

Seattle (ITC); (206) 527-3732

Spokane; (509) 358-7544

Tacoma; (206) 272-7232

Vancouver; (360) 260-6372

Walla Walla; (509) 527-4681

Wenatchee; (509) 662-8016

Yakima; (509) 574-4940

**Other Washington Resources**

Association of Washington Business
1414 S. Cherry St.
PO Box 658
Olympia, WA 98507-0658
(360) 943-1600

Small Business Administration
District Offices
1200 Sixth Ave., Ste. 1700
Seattle, WA 98101-1128
(206) 553-7310

W. 601 First Ave., 10th Fl.
Spokane, WA 99204-0317
(509) 353-2810

U.S. Dept. of Commerce District Offices
2001 Sixth Ave., Ste. 650
Seattle, WA 98121
(206) 553-5615

1020 W. Riverside Ave.
Spokane, WA 99201
(509) 624-1393

Internal Revenue Service
Seattle; (206) 442-1040
Elsewhere; (800) 829-1040

## WEST VIRGINIA

Development Office
Dept. of Commerce
Capitol Complex, Bldg. 6, Rm. 525
Charleston, WV 25305
(304) 558-2234

### Business Development

Guaranteed Work Force Program
(304) 558-2234

Small Business Development Center
(304) 558-2960

### Financial Assistance

West Virginia Economic Development
Authority
(304) 558-3650

### Rural Development

Local Capacity Development
(304) 558-2001

### Small Business Development Centers

West Virginia Development Office
950 Kanawha Blvd. E
Charleston, WV 25301
(304) 558-2960

Beckley; (304) 255-4022

Fairmont; (304) 367-4125

Huntington; (304) 696-6789

Montgomery; (304) 442-5501

Morgantown; (304) 293-5839

Parkersburg; (304) 424-8277

Shepherdstown; (304) 876-5261

Wheeling; (304) 233-5900, ext. 4206

### Other West Virginia Resources

West Virginia Chamber of Commerce
1314 Virginia St., E
PO Box 2789
Charleston, WV 25330-2789
(304) 342-1115

Small Business Administration
District Offices
550 Eagan St., Rm. 309
Charleston, WV 25301
(304) 347-5220

168 W. Main St., 6th Fl.
Clarksburg, WV 26301
(304) 623-5631

U.S. Dept. of Commerce District Office
405 Capitol St., Ste. 807
Charleston, WV 25301-1727
(304) 347-5123

Internal Revenue Service
(800) 829-1040

## WISCONSIN

Dept. of Development
123 W. Washington Ave.
PO Box 7970
Madison, WI 53707
(608) 266-1018 *or*
(800) 435-7287

### Business Development

Bureau of Business Development
(608) 266-9884

Bureau of Business and Industry
Services
(608) 267-0313

Manufacturing Assessment Center
(608) 266-0165

Permit Information Center
(608) 266-1018 *or*
(800) 435-7287

Small Business Ombudsman
(608) 267-9384

### Financial Assistance

Wisconsin Business Development
Finance Corp.
(608) 258-8830

Wisconsin Development Fund
(608) 266-1018

Wisconsin Housing and Economic
Development Authority
(800) 331-6873

### Minority/Women's Opportunities

Bureau of Minority Business
Development
(608) 267-9550

Women's Business Liaison
(608) 266-9944

Wisconsin Housing and Economic
Development Authority
(800) 334-6873

### Rural Development

Rural Economic Development Program
(608) 226-1018

### Small Business Development Centers

University of Wisconsin
432 N. Lake St., Rm. 423
Madison, WI 53706
(608) 263-7794

Eau Claire; (715) 836-5811

Green Bay; (414) 465-2089

Kenosha; (414) 595-2189

LaCrosse; (608) 785-8782

Madison; (608) 263-2221

Milwaukee; (414) 227-3240

Oshkosh; (414) 424-1453

Stevens Point; (715) 346-2004

Superior; (715) 394-8351

Whitewater; (414) 472-3217

**Other Wisconsin Resources**

Wisconsin Manufacturers
and Commerce
501 E. Washington Ave.
PO Box 352
Madison, WI 53701-0352
(608) 258-3400

Small Business Administration
District Offices
212 E. Washington Ave., Rm. 213
Madison, WI 53703
(608) 264-5261

310 W. Wisconsin Ave., Ste. 400
Milwaukee, WI 53203
(414) 297-3941

U.S. Dept. of Commerce District Office
517 E. Wisconsin Ave., Rm. 596
Milwaukee, WI 53202-4588
(414) 297-3473

Internal Revenue Service
Milwaukee; (414) 271-3780
Elsewhere; (800) 829-1040

## WYOMING

Division of Economic and Community
Development
6101 Yellowstone Rd., 4th Fl.
Cheyenne, WY 82002
(307) 777-7284

**Business Development**

DECD Business Development Section
(307) 777-7284

Business/Entrepreneur Assistance
(307) 777-7133

Mid-America Manufacturing Technology
Center
(307) 766-4811

**Financial Assistance**

Division of Economic Analysis
(307) 777-7504

Science, Technology and Energy
Authority
(307) 766-6797

Wyoming Industrial Development Corp.
(307) 234-5351

DECD Small Grants Program
(307) 777-7284

**Minority/Women's Opportunities**

Wyoming Dept. of Transportation
(307) 777-4457

**Rural Development**

Department of Agriculture,
Marketing Office
(307) 777-6581

**Small Business Development Centers**

University of Wyoming
PO Box 3622
Laramie, WY 82071-3622
(307) 766-3505 *or* (800) 348-5194

Casper; (307) 234-6683

Cheyenne; (307) 632-6141

Powell; (307) 754-2139

Rock Springs; (307) 352-6894

**Other Wyoming Resources**

Wyoming Dept. of Employment
(307) 777-7672

Small Business Administration
District Office
100 E. B St., Federal Bldg., Rm. 4001
PO Box 2839
Casper, WY 82602-2839
(307) 261-6500

U.S. Dept. of Commerce District Office
1625 Broadway, Ste. 680
Denver, CO 80202-4706
(303) 844-6622

Internal Revenue Service
(800) 829-1040

# Glossary

**Account**   (1) A record of a business transaction. (2) A contract arrangement, written or unwritten, to purchase and take delivery with payment to be made later as arranged.

**Account balance**   The difference between debits and credits relative to an account.

**Accountant**   One who is skilled at keeping business records. Usually a highly trained professional rather than one who keeps books. An accountant can set up the books needed for a business to operate and help the owner understand them.

**Accounting period**   A time interval at the end of which an accountant analyzes bookkeeping records. Also, the period covered by a profit-and-loss statement.

**Accounts payable**   Money owed for goods or services received but not yet paid for.

**Accounts receivable**   Money owed for goods or services delivered but not yet paid for.

**Accrual basis**   A method of keeping accounts that shows expenses incurred and income earned for a given fiscal period, even though such expenses are unpaid and income has not been received.

**Actuary**   An expert in pension and life insurance matters, trained in mathematical, statistical, and accounting methods and procedures.

**Administrative expense**   An expense chargeable to the managerial, general administrative, and policy phases of a business in contrast to sales, manufacturing, or cost-of-goods expense.

**Agent**   A person authorized to act for or represent another in dealing with a third party.

**Amortization**   To liquidate on an installment basis; the process of gradually paying off a liability over a period of time.

**Annual report**   The yearly report made by a company at the close of the fiscal year. States the company's receipts and disbursements, assets and liabilities.

**Appraisal**   (1) Evaluation of a specific piece of personal or real property. (2) The value placed on the property evaluated.

**Appreciation**   The increase in the value of an asset in excess of its depreciable cost due to economic or other conditions. Distinguished from increases in value due to improvements or additions made to it.

**Arrear**   (1) Amount past due and unpaid. (2) Being late in paying. Used in either sense, the term usually takes the plural form: in arrears.

**Asset**   Anything of worth that is owned by an individual, corporation, or other organization. Accounts receivable are an asset.

**Assign**   To transfer ownership of an asset to another party by signing a document.

**Audit**   An examination of accounting documents and supporting evidence.

**Bad debt**   Money owed that is expected to be uncollectible.

**Balance**   The amount of money remaining in an account.

**Balance sheet**   A financial statement showing assets on the left side and liabilities on the right. Provides an overview of a company's financial position at a given time.

**Balloon payment**   The last payment of a loan, significantly larger than previous installments, which pays off the loan in full.

**Bill of lading**   A document issued by a railroad or other carrier. Acknowledges the receipt of specified goods for transportation to a certain place, sets forth the contract between the shipper and the carrier, and helps ensure proper delivery of goods.

**Bill of sale**   A formal legal document conveying, from the seller to the buyer, title to or right or interest in specific personal property.

**Board of directors**   Individuals elected by stockholders to manage a corporation.

**Boilerplate**   Standardized language in a contract or other agreement.

**Bookkeeping**   Recording business transactions in the accounting records. The "books" are the documents in which the records of transactions are kept.

**Bottom line**   The figure that reflects company profitability on the income statement. The bottom line is the profit after all expenses and taxes have been paid.

**Brand**   A design, mark, symbol, or other device that distinguishes one line or type of goods from those of a competitor.

**Break-even point**   When total revenue equals total expenses. Above the break-even point, the business is making a profit. Below the break-even point, the business is incurring a loss.

**Broker**   Individual or company authorized to buy or sell something for another party, without ever owning the goods.

**Budget**   An estimate of the income and expenditures for a future period of time, usually one year.

**Business plan**   A detailed description of a new or existing business, including the company's product or service, marketing plan, financial statements and projections, and management principles.

**Capital**   (1) Money available to invest. (2) The total of accumulated assets available for production.

**Capital equipment**  Equipment used to manufacture a product; provide a service; or sell, store, or deliver merchandise. Such equipment will not be sold in the normal course of business; it will be used and worn out or consumed.

**Capital expenditure**  Purchase of long-term assets, especially equipment, used in manufacturing a product.

**Capital gain**  The difference between purchase price and selling price.

**Cash**  Money in hand or readily available.

**Cash discount**  A deduction given for prompt payment.

**Cash flow**  Incoming cash less outgoing cash during a given period.

**Cash receipt**  The money received by a business from customers.

**Certified development company (CDC)**  A local or statewide corporation or authority (for profit or nonprofit, depending on the situation) that packages Small Business Administration (SBA), bank, state, or private money into a financial assistance package for capital improvement of existing business. The SBA holds the second lien on its maximum share of 40 percent involvement. Each state has at least one CDC. The CDC program is also called the 504 Program.

**Certified lender**  A bank that participates in the Small Business Administration's (SBA's) guaranteed loan program, has a good track record with the SBA, and agrees to certain conditions. In return, the SBA agrees to process any guaranteed loan application within three business days. An SBA district office can provide a list of certified banks in the area.

**Certified public accountant (CPA)**  An accountant to whom a state has given a certificate showing that she or he has met prescribed requirements designed to ensure competence. Such an accountant is permitted to use the designation Certified Public Accountant, commonly abbreviated CPA.

**Chamber of Commerce**  A business-people's organization designed to advance the interests of its members. Comprises three levels: national, state, and local.

**Collateral**  Property or something of value offered to secure a loan or credit. Collateral becomes subject to seizure upon default.

**Commercial credit**  Short-term credit extended by a seller to the buyer to finance the purchase of a product or service.

**Commission**  A percentage of the principal or income an agent receives as compensation.

**Community Reinvestment Act (CRA)**  Act passed in 1977 to encourage banks to meet credit needs in their communities.

**Compensating balance**  Money left in a deposit account as part of a loan agreement.

**Compound interest**  Interest earned on previously accumulated interest as well as principal.

**Contract**   An agreement stating responsibilities between two or more parties.

**Controllable expense**   Expense that can be controlled or restrained.

**Corporation**   (1) A voluntary organization of persons, actual individuals or legal entities, legally bound together to form a business enterprise. (2) An artificial legal entity created by government grant and treated by law as an individual entity. Stockholders and the board of directors control both types.

**Cosigners**   Joint signers of a loan agreement. Cosigners pledge to meet the obligations of a business in case of default.

**Cost of goods sold**   The direct cost, to the business owner, of items to be sold to customers.

**CPA**   See Certified public accountant.

**CRA**   See Community Reinvestment Act.

**Credit**   Another word for debt. Credit is given to customers when they are allowed to make a purchase with the promise to pay later.

**Credit bureau**   A company that compiles and maintains information on consumer credit and provides information to potential creditors for a fee.

**Credit line**   The maximum amount of credit or money a financial institution or firm will extent.

**Credit rating**   An evaluation of an individual or corporation's history of repaying past loans. Credit ratings are used to assess the future ability of a creditor to pay back loans.

**Current asset**   Valuable resource or property that will be turned into cash or used up in the operation of the company within one year. Cash, accounts receivable, inventory, and prepaid expenses are usually current assets.

**Current liability**   Amount owed that will ordinarily be paid within one year. Accounts payable, the current portion of a long-term debt, and interest and dividends payable are usually current liabilities.

**Current ratio**   Current assets divided by current liabilities. Measures the ability of a company to pay its current obligations from current assets.

**Debenture**   Debt secured by a creditor based on the debtor's general creditworthiness. Distinguished from security based on specific assets.

**Debt**   That which is owed. Borrowed funds are considered debt and must generally be secured by collateral or a cosigner.

**Debt capital**   The part of investment capital that must be borrowed.

**Debt ratio**   Total liabilities divided by total liabilities plus capital. Measures the debt level of a business (average).

**Default**   (1) Failure of a borrower to make interest or principal payments when due. (2) Failure to meet an obligation.

**Deficit** A company's net loss when expenditures exceed income, or the excess of liabilities over assets. A negative net worth.

**Depreciation** A decrease in value through age, wear and tear, or deterioration. Depreciation is a normal expense of doing business and must be taken into account. Depreciation on business equipment is generally tax deductible.

**Direct loan** Financial assistance provided through the lending of federal money for a specific period of time, with a reasonable expectation of repayment. Such loans may or may not require the payment of interest.

**Direct mail** Using the mail to market goods or services directly to the consumer.

**Direct selling** The process whereby the producer sells to the user, ultimate customer, or retailer without an intermediary.

**Disaster loan** Physical or economic loan assistance available to individuals and businesses who have suffered loss due to natural disaster. This is the only Small Business Administration loan available for residential purposes.

**Disbursement** A payment made to satisfy a debt or other financial obligation.

**Distribution** Payment made to the owner(s) of an asset such as a stock or retirement fund.

**Distribution channel** The route a product follows as it moves from the original grower, producer, or importer to the ultimate consumer.

**Distributor** A wholesaler, agent, or company distributing goods to dealers or companies.

**Dividend** Earnings distributed to shareholders.

**Employer identification number** A number a business obtains from the Internal Revenue Service by filing Form SS-4. This number is to be shown on all business tax returns, documents, and statements. Wholesalers often request this number when offering wholesale prices to retailers.

**Entrepreneur** An innovator of business enterprise who recognizes opportunities to introduce a new product, process or organization and who raises the necessary money, assembles the factors for production, and organizes an operation to exploit the opportunity.

**Equal Credit Opportunity Act** Federal Reserve Regulation B, which prohibits lenders from denying an application on the basis of race, color, religion, national origin, sex, marital status, or age. Lenders are also prohibited from discouraging an applicant on such a basis.

**Equipment** Physical property of a more or less permanent nature ordinarily useful in carrying on operations. Land, buildings, and improvements are not equipment. Examples are furniture, machinery, tools, and vehicles.

**Equity** (1) A financial investment in a business. An equity investment carries with it a share of ownership, a stake in profits, and a say in management. Equity is calculated by subtracting liabilities from assets. (2) In banking, the difference between the market value of an asset and the amount of claims (such as mortgages) against it. (3) In investing, financing by means of shareholders' investments, usually stock purchases. Equity financing is the major alternative to debt financing (borrowing).

**Equity capital** Money furnished by business owners.

**Escrow** The temporary deposit of assets with a third party. The money is released when specified conditions have been met.

**Extraordinary item** Unusual or nonrecurring event that must be explained to shareholders.

**Factoring** A type of financing in which receivables are assigned to a factoring company responsible for collecting them.

**Fiscal year** Any twelve-month period used by a company or government as an accounting period.

**Fixed asset** Land, building, equipment, etc. of a lasting nature and not usually converted into cash in the course of doing business.

**Fixed expense** A cost that does not vary from one period to the next. Generally, fixed expenses are unaffected by the volume of business. The cost of a leased computer is a fixed expense.

**Franchise** A business involving three elements: a franchise fee, the allocation of rights, and a continuous relationship with the parent company.

**Grace period** The time allowed before a creditor initiates legal action.

**Gross profit** The difference between the selling price and the cost of an item. Gross profit is calculated by subtracting cost of goods sold from net sales or revenues before consideration of operating expenses.

**Guarantee** A third party's pledge to repay a loan in the event that a borrower cannot.

**Guaranteed loan** Programs in which the federal government makes an arrangement to indemnify a lender against part or all of any defaults by those responsible for repayment of loans.

**Income statement** *See* Profit and loss statement.

**Incubator** A facility in which fledgling enterprises share services. Shared services may include meeting areas; library, secretarial, and accounting resources; and financial and management counselors.

**Indemnity** The obligation of one party to reimburse another for real or possible losses.

**Industrial development authority** Political entity established to finance economic development in an area, usually through loans to nonprofit organizations that, in turn, provide facilities for manufacturing or industrial operations.

**Interest** The cost of borrowing money.

**Inventory**   The value of raw materials, work in process, supplies used in operations, and finished goods.

**Keystone**   To set a retail price that is twice the wholesale price.

**Lease**   A long-term rental agreement.

**Ledger**   The record of income and expenditures.

**Leverage**   Incurring debt in order to continue or expand the scope of a business operation. An enterprise is said to be highly leveraged if it relies heavily on debt financing as opposed to equity financing.

**Liability**   In business, any obligation to pay another party now or in the future.

**Liability insurance**   Risk protection for actions for which a business is liable.

**Lien**   The legal right to hold or sell the property of another as a guarantee against nonpayment.

**Limited partnership**   A legal partnership in which owners assume responsibility only up to the amount invested.

**Line of credit**   A financial institution's promise to lend up to a specific amount during a specific time.

**Liquid asset**   An asset that is easily convertible to cash.

**Liquidate**   To settle a debt or to convert to cash.

**Liquidation**   The sale of assets to pay debts.

**Liquidity**   (1) The ability to meet financial responsibilities. (2) The degree of readiness with which assets can be converted into cash without a loss.

**Loan**   Money lent with interest.

**Loan agreement**   A document that states what a business can and cannot do as long as it owes money to the lender.

**Local development corporation**   An organization, usually made up of local citizens, designed to improve the economy of an area by inducing business and industry to locate there. A local development corporation usually has financing capabilities.

**Long-term liability**   A liability (expense) that will not mature within one year.

**Management**   The art of conducting and supervising a business.

**Marginal cost**   Additional cost associated with producing one more unit of output.

**Market niche**   A well-defined group of customers for whom your product or service is particularly suitable.

**Marketing**   All the activities involved in buying and selling a product or service.

**Merchandise**   Goods bought and sold or waiting in inventory.

**Microbusiness**   An owner-operated business with few employees and less than $250,000 in annual sales.

**Middleman**   A person or company that performs functions or renders services involved in the purchase or sale of goods in their flow from producer to consumer.

**Minority business**   According to the Small Business Administration (SBA), businesses whose owners are "socially and economically disadvantaged." Social disadvantage pertains to membership in one of several different racial or ethnic categories defined by 13CFR, Part 124 or as established on a case-by-case basis by others (such as those with physical disabilities). Economic disadvantage pertains to barriers that social disadvantage places in the way of an individual's participation in business and employment. SBA district office specialists can help with definitions. In most cases, women do not qualify for minority status on the basis of their sex alone.

**Multilevel selling**   Selling through thousands of independent distributors. Multilevel sales companies offer distributors commissions on both retail sales and the sales of their downline (the network of other distributors they sponsor). Multilevel selling is also known as network marketing.

**Net**   What is left after deducting all expenses from the gross income. Net is also called net income.

**Net worth**   The total value of a business in financial terms. Calculated by subtracting total liabilities from total assets.

**Network marketing**   *See* Multilevel selling.

**Nonbank lenders**   Any commercial lender not classified as a bank. Examples include investment companies, savings and loan associations, credit unions, lending units of major corporations (for example, AT&T Capital, General Motors Accep-

tance Corp., GE Capital), mortgage companies, venture capitalists, development corporations, insurance companies, and independent lenders (for example, Money Store).

**Nonrecurring**   One time, not repeating. Nonrecurring expenses are those involved in starting a business.

**Note**   A document that is recognized as legal evidence of a debt.

**Office of Small and Disadvantaged Business Utilization**   An office within each agency of the federal government. Has significant procurement authority and ensures agency compliance with federal regulations requiring the purchase of a certain percentage of products and services from small and minority businesses.

**Operating cost**   (1) An expenditure arising out of current business activities. (2) The cost incurred to do business: salary, electricity, rent. Also called overhead.

**Operating expense**   A cost associated with the day-to-day activities of a business.

**Operating profit (or loss)**   Income (or loss) before deduction of taxes and extraordinary items (those resulting from transactions outside the normal course of business).

**Outsource**   To obtain components or services from outside suppliers.

**Overhead**   A general term for cost of materials and services not directly adding to or readily identifiable with the product or service being sold. *See also* Operating cost.

**Partnership** A company owned by two or more people who are jointly and personally liable for debts and assets of the company. General partners, who have control, have unlimited liability; limited partners have limited liability.

**Payable** Ready to be paid. *See also* Accounts payable.

**Preferred lender** A bank with a special written agreement with the Small Business Administration (SBA). The agreement allows the bank to make a guaranteed SBA loan without prior SBA approval. Preferred loans have a maximum SBA guarantee of 75 percent.

**Prepaid expense** An expenditure for items not yet received.

**Prime rate** The interest rate that banks charge their best commercial customers. Rates charged to other borrowers are often expressed in terms of the prime rate plus a specified number of percentage points.

**Principal** The amount of money borrowed in a debt agreement and the amount upon which interest is calculated.

**Pro forma** An estimate of what may result in the future from actions in the present. A pro forma financial statement shows how the actual operations of the business will turn out if certain assumptions prove correct.

**Profit** Financial gain; returns over expenditures.

**Profit and loss statement** A list of the total amount of sales (revenues) and total costs (expenses). Also called an income statement.

**Profit margin** The difference between selling price and all costs.

**Prompt pay** Payment, by federal agencies, within 45 days of billing. If federal agencies do not pay within 45 days, they have to pay interest on the overdue amount.

**Psychographics** The study of psychological factors that affect the purchasing patterns of consumers.

**Receivable** *See* Accounts receivable.

**Receivable financing** The type of financing in which a business borrows money with the expectation of repaying it quickly, upon receipt of certain receivables. The receivables are pledged as collateral on the loan.

**Retail** To sell directly to the consumer.

**Retained earning** Net profit kept in a business after dividends are paid.

**Revenue** Total sales during a stated period.

**SBIC** *See* Small Business Investment Company.

**Security** Collateral promised to a lender as protection in case of default.

**Service business** A retail business that performs activities that benefit others.

**Service Corps of Retired Executives (SCORE)** A management assistance program of the Small Business Administration (SBA). SCORE volunteers provide one-on-one counseling, workshops, and seminars for small firms.

**Share** One of the equal parts into which the ownership of a corporation is divided.

**Short-term note** A loan that comes due in one year or less.

**Simple interest** Interest paid only on the principal of a loan. No interest is paid on interest accrued during the term of the loan.

**Small business** Generally, a business that has fewer than five hundred employees and is not dominant in its field. For lending purposes, the Small Business Administration defines the size of a business according to industry-specific standard guidelines that cite number of employees or average annual receipts.

**Small Business Investment Company (SBIC)** An SBIC is licensed by the Small Business Administration as a federally funded private venture-capital firm. An SBIC makes money available to small businesses under a variety of agreements. This money is typically for capital expansion for new, risky, or high-tech firms.

**Sole proprietorship** A business structure in which the owner has full control and unlimited liability.

**Speculation** The purchase of an asset with the expectation of selling it quickly for a large gain.

**Stock** (1) An ownership share in a corporation; another name for a share. (2) Accumulated merchandise, ready for sale.

**Surety bond** A bond that provides reimbursement to an individual or company if a firm fails to complete a contract. The Small Business Administration can guarantee surety bonds.

**Target market** The specific individuals who are potential customers.

**Tax number** A number assigned to a business, by a state revenue department, that enables the business to buy wholesale without paying sales tax. Contact the state department of revenue for information.

**Telemarketing** Marketing goods or services directly to the consumer via the telephone.

**Terms of sale** The conditions concerning payment for a purchase.

**Trade credit** Permission to buy from suppliers on open account.

**Variable cost** Any cost that changes significantly with the level of output.

**Venture capital** Money used to purchase an equity stake in a new or existing enterprise.

**Wholesale** Selling for resale.

**Working capital** The excess of current assets over current liabilities. The cash needed to keep the business running from day to day.

# Recommended Reading

## CHAPTER ONE

Abarbanel, Karin. *How to Succeed On Your Own: Overcoming the Emotional Roadblocks on the Way From Corporation to Cottage, From Employee to Entrepreneur*. New York: Henry Holt, 1994.

Anderson, Nancy. *Work with Passion: How to Do What You Love for a Living*. San Rafael, California: New World Library, 1993.

Attard, Janet. *The Home Office and Small Business Answer Book: Solutions to Most Frequently Asked Questions About Starting and Running Home Offices and Small Businesses*. New York: Henry Holt, 1993.

Baker, Sunny and Kim. *Million Dollar Home-Based Businesses: Successful Entrepreneurs who Have Built Substantial Enterprises from Their Homes*. Chicago: Adams Publishing, 1993.

Berner, Jeff. *The Joy of Working from Home: Making a Life While Making a Living*. New York: Barrett Koehler Publishing, 1994.

Chandler, Arline. *Road Work: The Ultimate RVing Adventure*. Heber Springs, Arkansas: Flying Horse Press, 1997.

Cochrane, Patrick. *The Kitchen Table Millionaire: Home-Based Money-Making Strategies to Build Financial Independence Today*. Rockland California: Prima Publishing, 1997.

Edwards, Paul and Sarah. *Finding Your Perfect Work*. A Jeremy P, Tarcher/Putnam Book, 1996.

———— *Working from Home: Everything You Need to Know about Living and Working Under the Same Roof*. New York: Putnam Publishing Group, 1994.

Fisher, Lionel L. *On Your Own: A Guide to Working Happily, Productively and Successfully from Home*. Englewood Cliffs, New Jersey, Prentice-Hall Trade, 1994.

Folger, Liz. *The Stay-At-Home Mom's Guide to Making Money: How to Create the Business That's Right for You Using the Skills and Interests You Already Have*. Rockland, California: Prima Publishing, 1997.

Fox, Marcia, Ph.D., Editor. *Be Your Own Business! The Definitive Guide to Entrepreneurial Success*. Indianapolis, Indiana, Jist Works, 1997.

Fuller, Cheri. *Home Business Happiness*. Starburst Publishers, Lancaster, Pennsylvania, 1996.

Gray, Douglas A. *The Entrepreneur's Complete Self-Assessment Guide*. Vancouver, British Columbia: Self-Counsel Press, 1990.

Gregory, Scott and Shirley. *The Home Team: How Couples Can Make a Life and a Living Working at Home*. New York: Panda Publishing, 1997.

Holland, Philip. *How to Start a Business Without Quitting Your Job: The Moonlight Entrepreneur's Guide*. Berkeley, California: Ten Speed Press, 1992.

Hucknall, Nanette V. *Finding Your Work, Loving Your Life*. York Beach, Maine: Samuel Weiser, Inc., 1992.

Leboeuf, Michael. *The Perfect Business: How to Make a Million from Home with No Payroll, No Employee Headaches, No Debts and No Sleepless Nights!* New York: Fireside, 1996.

Murray, Katherine. *Home but Not Alone: The Work-At-Home Parents' Handbook*. Indianapolis, Indiana: Jist Works, 1997.

Naisbitt, John, and Patricia Aburdene. *Megatrends 2000*. New York: Avon Books, 1996.

Oberlin, Loriann Hoff. *Working at Home While the Kids Are There, Too*. Chicago: Career Press, 1997.

Parlapiano, Ellen H. and Patricia Cobe. *Mompreneurs: A Mother's Practical Step-By-Step Guide to Work-At-Home Success*. New York: Perigee/Berkley, 1996.

Partow, Cameron and Donna. *How to Work with the One You Love and Live to Tell About It*. Bloomington, Minnesota: Bethany House, 1995.

Peterson, Joe and Kay. *Travel While You Work*. Livingston, Texas: RoVer's Publications, 1997.

Popcorn, Faith. *Clicking: 16 Trends to Future-Fit Your Life, Your Work and Your Business*. New York: Harper Business Books, Inc., 1996.

Roberts, Lisa. *How To Raise a Family and a Career Under One Roof*. Moon Township, Pennsylvania: Bookhaven Press, 1997.

Ross, Tom and Marilyn. *Country Bound: Trade Your Business Suit Blues for Blue Jean Dreams*. Buena Vista, Colorado, Communication Creativity, 1992.

Tarkenton, Fran and Wes Smith. *What Losing Taught Me About Winning: The Ultimate Guide for Success in Small and Home-Based Business*. New York: Simon & Schuster, 1997.

Winter, Barbara J. *Making a Living Without a Job: Winning Ways for Creating Work That You Love*. New York: Bantam Doubleday Dell Publishing, 1993.

## CHAPTER TWO

Allen, S. Carol. *The Complete Business Guide for a Profitable Internet, BBS, Online Service*. Yucca Valley, California: InfoLink, 1995.

Appelbaum, Judith. *How to Get Happily Published—A Complete and Candid Guide*. New York: Harper Collins, 1992.

Arden, Lynie. *101 Franchises You Can Run from Home*. New York: John Wiley & Sons, 1990.

Argyle, Carolyn. *How to Start and Run a Home Day-Care Business*. New York: Citadel Press, 1997.

Aslett, Don and Mark Browning. *Cleaning Up for a Living: Everything You Need to Know to Become a Successful Building Service Contractor*. Crozet, Virginia: Betterway Publications, 1991.

Avila-Weil, Donna CMT and Mary Glaccum CMT. *The Independent Medical Transcriptionist*. Windsor, California: Rayve Productions Inc., 1997.

———— and Wanda Regan CCS. *Independent Medical Coding*, Windsor, California: Rayve Productions Inc., 1997.

Benzel, Rick. *Making Money in a Health Service Business on Your Home-Based PC*. Blue Ridge Summit, Pennsylvania: McGraw Hill, 1997.

———— and Katherine Sheehy Hussey, *Legal and Paralegal Services on Your Home-Based PC*. Blue Ridge Summit, Pennsylvania: Windcrest, 1994.

Bly, Robert W. *Getting Your Book Published: Inside Secrets of a Successful Author*. New York, Henry Holt and Company, 1997.

———— *Secrets of a Freelance Writer: How to Make $85,000 Dollars a Year*. New York: Henry Holt and Company, 1997.

———— *Start and Run a Profitable Mail-Order Business: Getting Started for Under $500*. Vancouver, British Columbia: Self Counsel Press, 1997.

Bond, William J. *Going Solo: Developing a Home-Based Consulting Business from the Ground Up*. Blue Ridge Summit, Pennsylvania: McGraw Hill, 1997.

———— *Home-Based Catalog Marketing*. New York: Tab/McGraw Hill, 1993.

———— *Home-Based Mail Order*. New York: Tab/McGraw Hill, 1990.

———— *Home-Based Newsletter Publishing*. New York: McGraw Hill, 1991.

Boyce, Susan M., et al. *Writing Travel Books and Articles*. Vancouver, British Columbia,: Self-Counsel Press, 1997.

Brabec, Barbara. *Creative Cash—How to Sell Your Crafts, Needlework Designs and Know-How*. Cincinnati, Ohio: Barbara Brabec Productions, 1993.

———— *Homemade Money: How to Select, Start, Manage, Market and Multiply the Profits of a Business at Home*. Cincinnati, Ohio: Betterway Publications, 1997.

Braidwood, Barbara, Susan M. Boyce and Richard Cropp. *Start & Run a Profitable Tour Guiding Business: Part-Time, Full-Time, at Home or Abroad*. Bellingham, Washington: Self-Counsel Press, 1996.

Brodsky, Bart, and Janet Geis. *The Teaching Marketplace: Make Money with Freelance Teaching, Corporate Training, and on the Lecture Circuit*. New York: Community Resource Institute Press, 1991.

Bryant, Alan D. *Creating Successful Bulletin Board Systems*. Reading, Massachusetts: Addison Wesley, 1994.

Burstiner, Irving. *Start & Run Your Own Profitable Service Business*. Englewood Cliffs, New Jersey: Prentice Hall Trade, 1992.

Caputo, Kathryn. *The Selling from Home Sourcebook*. Cincinnati, Ohio: Betterway Books, 1996.

Clark, Beverly. *Planning a Wedding to Remember*. Los Angeles: Wilshire Publications, 1995.

Culligan, Joseph J. *You, Too, Can Find Anybody*. Miami, Florida: FJA Inc., 1995.

David, Bernard J. *The Entrepreneurial PC: The Complete Guide to Starting a PC-Based Business*. Blue Ridge Summit, Pennsylvania: Windcrest, 1993.

Davies, Mary F., Pat Hardy, Joanne M. Bell, and Susan Brown. *So You Want to Be an Innkeeper*. San Francisco: Chronicle Books, 1996.

Dearing, James. *Making Money Making Music (No Matter Where You Live)*. Cincinnati, Ohio: Writer's Digest, 1990.

Dell, Owen E. *How to Start a Home-Based Landscaping Business*. Old Saybrook, Connecticut: Globe Pequot Press, 1997.

Denton, Lynn and Jody Kelly. *Designing, Writing and Producing Computer Documentation*. New York: McGraw-Hill, 1993.

DeWalt, Suzanne. *How to Start a Home-Based Interior Design Business*. Old Saybrook, Connecticut: Globe Pequot Press, 1997.

Dillehay, James. *Weaving Profits: How to Make Money Selling Your Handwovens (or Any Other Crafts)*. Torreon, New Mexico: Warm Snow Publishers, 1992.

Dorsheimer, Wesley. *The Newsletter Handbook*. New York: Hippocrene Books, 1993.

Edwards, Paul and Sarah. *Making Money with Your Computer at Home: The Inside Information You Need to Know to Select and Operate a Full-Time, Part-Time or Add-On Business*. New York: Jeremy P. Tarcher, 1997.

Edwards, Paul and Sarah and Walter Zooi. *Home Businesses You Can Buy: The Definitive Guide to Exploring Franchises, Multi-Level Marketing and Business Opportunities, And Avoiding Scams*. New York: Putnam Publishing Group, 1997.

Entrepreneur Magazine: *Making Money with Your Personal Computer*. New York: John Wiley & Sons, 1995.

Erdosh, George. *Start and Run a Profitable Catering Business: From Thyme to Timing*. Vancouver, British Columbia: Self-Counsel Press, 1994.

Fife, Bruce, et al. *Creative Clowning*. New York: Piccadilly Books, 1992.

——— *Make Money Reading Books! How to Start and Operate Your Own Home-Based Freelance Reading Service*. New York: Piccadilly Books, 1993.

Fiumara, Georganne. *How to Start a Home-Based Mail-Order Business*. Old Saybrook, Connecticut: Globe Pequot Press, 1996.

Floyd, Elaine. *Making Money Writing Newsletters: From Moonlighting to Full-Time Work, How to Set Up and Run a Newsletter Production Service*. St. Louis, Missouri: E.F. Communications, 1994.

Fox, Jack. *Starting and Building Your Own Accounting Business*. New York: John Wiley & Sons, 1996.

Foster-Walker, Mardi, *Start and Run a Profitable Gift Basket Business*. Vancouver, British Columbia: Self Counsel Press, 1995.

Frazier, Shirley George. *How to Start a Home-Based Gift Basket Business*. Old Saybrook, Connecticut: Globe Pequot Press, 1998.

Gallagher, Patricia C. *Start Your Own At-Home Child Care Business*. St. Louis, Missouri: Mosby-Year Book, 1994.

Glenn, Peggy. *Word Processing Profits at Home: A Complete Business Plan*. Huntington Beach, California: Aames-Allen Publishing, 1994.

Gluck, Nancy DeProspo. *Affairs of the Heart: How to Start and Operate a Successful Special Event Planning Service*. Lanoka Harbor New Jersey: Humbug Associates Inc., 1993.

Hagan, Louise. *Start and Run a Profitable Office Service Business from Your Home*. Vancouver, British Columbia: Self-Counsel Press, 1995.

Hall, Stephen F. *From Kitchen to Market: Selling Your Gourmet Food Specialty*. Chicago, Illinois, Upstart Publishing Company, 1992.

Harrison, Henry S. *Appraising Residences and Income Properties*. New Haven Connecticut: H2 Co., 1989.

Hawkins, Nan Lee, et al. *Profitable Child Care; How to Start and Run a Successful Business*. New York: Facts on File, 1993.

Holtz, Herman. *The Complete Guide to Being an Independent Contractor*. Dover, New Hampshire: Upstart Publications, 1995.

——— Herman. *Computer Consulting on Your Home-Based PC*. Blue Ridge Summitt, Pennsylvania: Windcrest, 1994.

——— Herman. *How to Start and Run a Writing and Editing Business*. New York: John Wiley & Sons, 1992.

Hordeski, Michael F. *Repairing PCs: Beyond the Basics*. Blue Ridge Summit, Pennsylvania: Windcrest, 1994.

Kent, Peter. *Making Money in Technical Writing*. New York: Arco Publishing, 1997.

Keup, Erwin J., *The Franchise Bible: How to Buy a Franchise or Franchise Your Own Business*, Grants Pass, Oregon: Oasis Press/PSI Research, 1995.

Kilgore, Dawn, ed. *Start Your Own Childcare Business*. Englewood Cliffs, New Jersey: Prentice Hall Trade, 1996.

Kishel, Gregory and Patricia. *Build Your Own Network Sales Business*, New York: John Wiley & Sons, 1992.

———— *Network Marketing: Profiting From the People-Multi-Level Selling Method of the 1990s*. New York: John Wiley & Sons, 1991.

Krieff, Allan. *How to Start and Run Your Own Advertising Agency*. Blue Ridge Summit, Pennsylvania: McGraw-Hill, 1993.

Kursmark, Louise. *How to Start a Home-Based Desktop Publishing Business*. Old Saybrook, Connecticut: Globe-Pequot Press, 1996.

Landman, Sylvia. *Crafting for Dollars*. Rockland, California: Prima Publications, 1996.

Lant, Jeffery. *How to Make a Whole Lot More Than $1,000, 000 Writing, Commissioning, Publishing and Selling "How-To " Information*. New York: Jeffrey Lant Associates, 1990.

———— *Money Talks: The Complete Guide to Creating a Profitable Workshop or Seminar in Any Field*. New York: Jeffrey Lant Associates, 1992.

———— *Multi-Level Money: The Complete Guide to Generating, Closing and Working with All the People You Need to Make Real Money Every Month in Network Marketing*. New York: Jeffrey Lant Associates, 1995.

Lewis, Carol S., Harry L. Helms. *On Your Own: How to Escape the Corporation and Make More Money as an Independent Contractor*. New York: Hightext Publications, 1994.

Laurence, Robert. *Going Freelance: A Guide for Professionals*. New York; John Wiley and Sons, 1988.

Mancuso, Joseph. *Mancuso's Small Business Basics: Start, Buy or Franchise Your Way to a Successful Business*. New York: Sourcebooks Trade, 1997.

———— and Donald Boraian, *How to Buy and Manage a Franchise: The Definitive Resource Guide If You're Thinking of Purchasing a Franchise or Turning Your Business into One*. New York: Simon and Schuster, 1993.

Mariotti, Richard and Bruce Fife: *How to Be a Literary Agent*. New York: Piccadilly, 1996.

Masie, Elliott and Rebekah Wolman. *The Computer Training Handbook: Strategies for Helping People to Learn Technology*. Raquett Lake, New York: Masie Institute, 1995.

Maslowski, Karen L. *Sew up a Storm: All the Way to the Bank*. New York: Sewstorm, 1995.

Massie, Gabriele. *Employ Your PC: Businesses That Can Be Run from Home; Put Your Computer to Work for You*. New York: Red Tail Publishing, 1996.

Mastin, Robert. *900 Know-How: How to Succeed With Your Own 900 Number Business.* New York: Aegis Publishing Group, 1996.

Melnik, Jan. *How to Start a Home-Based Résumé Business.* Old Saybrook, Connecticut: Globe Pequot Press, 1997.

——— *How to Start a Home-Based Secretarial Services Business.* Old Saybrook, Connecticut: Globe Pequot Press, 1997.

Modigliani, Kathy. *Opening Your Door to Children.* Washington, D.C.: National Association for the Education of Young Children, 1987.

Neff, Jack. *Make Your Woodworking Pay for Itself.* Cincinnati, Ohio: Betterway Books, 1996.

Nicholas, Ted. *The Golden Mailbox: How to Get Rich Direct Marketing Your Product.* Chicago: Dearborn, 1992.

Monaghan, Kelly. *Home-Based Travel Agent.* New York: The Intrepid Traveler, 1997.

Norris, Shell and Judy. *Reunion!* (Software). Skokie, Illinois: Class Reunion, 1996.

Notarius, Barbara, Frederick G. Harmon and Gail Sforza Breuer. *Open Your Own Bed and Breakfast.* New York: John Wiley & Sons, 1996.

Oberrecht, Kenn. *How to Start a Home-Based Craft Business.* Old Saybrook, Connecticut: Globe-Pequot Press, 1997.

——— *How to Start a Home-Based Photography Business.* Old Saybrook, Connecticut: Globe Pequot Press, 1996.

Park, Robert. *The Inventor's Handbook: How to Develop, Protect and Market Your Invention.* Cincinnati, Ohio: Betterway Books, 1990.

Parker, Lucy. *How to Start a Home-Based Writing Business.* Old Saybrook, Connecticut: Globe Pequot Press, 1997.

Peake, Jacquelyn. *How to Start a Home-Based Antiques Business.* Old Saybrook, Connecticut: Globe Pequot Press, 1997.

Peters, Ellie Roosli. *Home Child Care: The Tender Business.* South Bend, Indiana: Greenlawn Press, 1990.

Powers, Mike. *How to Start a Mail Order Business.* New York: Avon Books, 1996.

Poynter, Dan. *Expert Witness Handbook: Tips and Techniques for the Litigation Consultant.* New York: Para Publishing, 1997.

Poynter, Dan. *The Self-Publishing Manual-How to Write, Print and Sell Your Own Book.* New York: Para Publishing, 1996.

Ramsey, Dan. *Electrical Contractor: Start and Run a Money-Making Business.* New York: Tab Books, 1993.

——— and Walter Curtis. *Painting Contractor: Start and Run a Money-Making Business.* New York: Tab Books, 1993.

———— *The Upstart Guide to Owning and Managing a Consulting Service.* Dover, New Hampshire: Upstart Press, 1995.

———— *The Upstart Guide to Owning and Managing a Desktop Publishing Business.* Dover, New Hampshire: Upstart Press, 1994.

———— *The Upstart Guide to Owning and Managing a Mail-Order Business.* New York: Tab Books, 1995.

———— *The Upstart Guide to Owning and Managing a Résumé Service.* Dover, New Hampshire: Upstart Press, 1994.

———— *The Upstart Guide to Owning and Managing a Travel Service.* Dover, New Hampshire: Upstart Press, 1995.

Richards, Judy. *Catering: Start and Run a Money-Making Business.* Blue Ridge Summit, Pennsylvania: McGraw-Hill, 1994.

Rogak, Lisa Angowski. *The Upstart Guide to Owning and Managing a Bed and Breakfast.* Dover, New Hampshire: Upstart Publishing Co., 1994.

Rohrbough, Linda, *Mailing List Services on Your Home-Based P.C.* Blue Ridge Summit, Pennsylvania: Windcrest, 1993.

Rohrbough, Linda and Michael Hordeski. *Start Your Own PC Repair Business.* Blue Ridge Summit, Pennsylvania: McGraw-Hill, 1995.

Ross, Marilyn, and Tom. *The Complete Guide to Self-Publishing—Everything You Need to Know to Write, Publish, Promote, and Sell Your Own Book.* Cincinnati, Ohio: Writer's Digest Books, 1994.

Rugge, Sue and Alfred Glossbrenner. *The Information Broker's Handbook.* Blue Ridge Summit, Pennsylvania: Windcrest, 1997.

Ruhl, Janet. *The Computer Consultant's Guide: Real Life Strategies for Building a Successful Consulting Career.* New York: John Wiley & Sons, 1997.

Rust, Herbert, *Owning Your Own Franchise*, New York: Prentice Hall, 1991.

Self, Charles, *How to Start a Home-Based Carpentry Business.* Old Saybrook, Connecticut: Globe Pequot Press, 1997.

Shaw, Lisa Angowski Rogak. *How to Make Money Publishing from Home: Everything You Need to Know to Successfully Publish Books, Newsletters, Greeting Cards, Zines and Software.* Rockland, California: Prima Publishing, 1997.

Shenson, Howard L. *How to Develop and Promote Successful Seminars and Workshops.* New York, John Wiley & Sons, 1990.

Shenson, Howard, Paul Franklin and Ted Nichols. *The Complete Guide to Consulting Success.* Chicago, Illinois: Upstart Press, 1997.

Shivell, Kirk and Kent Banning. *Running a Successful Franchise: The Nuts and Bolts Guide to Owning and Running a Franchise Business*, New York: McGraw-Hill, 1995.

Silliphant, Leigh and Sureleigh. *Making $70,000+ a Year as a Self-Employed Manufacturer's Representative*. Berkeley, California: Ten Speed Press, 1988.

Simon, Alan R. *How to Be a Successful Computer Consultant*. Blue Ridge Summit, Pennsylvania: McGraw-Hill, 1997.

Spike, Kathleen. *Sew to Success: How to Make Money in a Home-Based Sewing Business*. New York: Palmer Pletch Publishing, 1995.

Stankus, Jan. *How to Open and Operate a Bed and Breakfast*. Old Saybrook, Connecticut: Globe Pequot Press, 1997.

*Start Your Own Money Making Computer Business*, San Diego, California: Pfeiffer & Co., 1994.

Stellsmith-Duffin, Shari. *How to Start a Home-Based Day-Care Business*. Old Saybrook, Connecticut: Globe Pequot Press, 1997.

Stewart, Joyce. *How to Make Your Design Business Profitable*. Cincinnati, Ohio: North Light Books, 1992.

Sturdivant, Lee. *Herbs for Sale*. Friday Harbor, Washington: San Juan Naturals, 1994.

———— *Flowers for Sale: Growing and Marketing Cut Flowers—Backyard to Small Acreage; A Bootstrap Guide*. Friday Harbor, Washington; San Juan Naturals, 1994.

Summers, Harvey. *Operating a Desktop Video Service on Your Home-Based PC*. Blue Ridge Summit, Pennsylvania: McGraw-Hill, 1994.

Sykes, Barbara Wright. *The Business of Sewing*. Chino Hills, California: Collins Publications, 1992.

Taylor, Monica and Richard. *Start and Run a Profitable Bed and Breakfast*. Vancouver, B.C.: Self Counsel Press, 1992.

Taylor, Ted. *Secrets to a Successful Greenhouse Business*. Melbourne Florida: Greenearth Publishing, 1994

Tomzack, Mary E., *Tips and Traps When Buying a Franchise*, New York: McGraw-Hill, 1994.

Tooley, Michael. *Servicing Personal Computers*. Stoneham, Massachusetts: Butterworth-Heinemann, 1993.

Ventolo, William L. Jr. and Martha R. Williams. *Fundamentals of Real Estate Appraisal*. Chicago: Dearborn, 1997.

Vivaldo, Denise. *How to Start a Home-Based Catering Business*. Old Saybrook, Connecticut: Globe Pequot Press, 1996.

Walford, Lynn. *Make Money with Your PC!: The Revised Guide to Starting and Running Successful Businesses with Your Personal Computer*. Berkeley, California: Ten Speed Press, 1994.

Warner, Ralph E. *The Independent Parale-gal's Handbook: How to Provide Legal Services Without Becoming a Lawyer*. Berkeley: Nolo Press, 1996.

Weiss, Alan. *Million-Dollar Consulting*. New York: McGraw-Hill, 1994.

—— *Money Talks: How to Make a Million as a Speaker*, New York: McGraw-Hill, 1997.

Weiss, Kenneth. *Building an Import/Export Business*. New York: John Wiley & Sons, 1997.

Werksma, Louann Nagy. *How to Start a Home-Based Communications Business*. Old Saybrook, Connecticut: Globe Pequot Press, 1997.

—— *How to Start a Home-Based Public Relations Business*. Old Saybrook, Connecticut: Globe Pequot Press, 1997.

Whatley, Booker T. and the Editors of The New Farm. *How to Make $100,000 Farming 25 Acres*. Emmaus, Pennsylvania: Rodale Press, 1987.

Wilcox, Phil. *How to Earn More Than $25,000 a Year With Your Home Computer: Over 140 Income-producing Projects*. New York: Citadel Press, 1997.

Wilson, Sandi. *Be the Boss II: Running a Successful Service Business*. New York. Avon Books, 1993.

Wirths, Wally. *Your Field of Dreams: Making Money on Your Land*. New York: John Culler & Sons, 1997.

## CHAPTER 3

Abrams, Rhonda M. *The Successful Business Plan: Secrets & Strategies*. Grants Pass, Oregon: Oasis Press, 1992.

Baker, Sunny and Kim Baker. *Market Mapping*. New York: McGraw-Hill, 1993.

Bangs, David H., Jr. *The Business Planning Guide: Creating a Plan for Success in Your Own Business*. Dover, New Hampshire: Upstart Books, 1995.

Dorff, Pat, Edith Fine, and Judith Josephson. *File . . . Don't Pile!: For People Who Write: Handling the Paper Flow in the Workplace or Home Office*. New York: St. Martin's Press, 1994.

Eyler, David R. *Home Business Bible*. New York: John Wiley & Sons, Inc., 1994.

Fisher, Murray. *Working Alone: Words of Wisdom for the Self-Employed*. New York: Berkley Publishing Group, 1994.

Fishman, Stephen. *The Copyright Handbook: How to Protect and Use Written Works*. Berkeley, California: Nolo Press, 1997.

—— *Wage Slave No More: The Independent Contractor's Legal Guide*. Berkeley, California: Nolo Press, 1997.

Fox, Jack, *Accounting and Recordkeeping Made Easy for the Self-Employed*. New York: John Wiley & Sons, Inc., 1994..

Frigsted, David P. *Know Your Market: How To Do Low-Cost Market Research*. Grants Pass, Oregon: Oasis Press, 1995.

Gilkerson, Linda and Theresia Paauwe. *Self-Employment: From Dream to Reality; Business Planning for Microenterprises.* Indianapolis, Indiana: Jist Works, 1997.

Gray, Douglas A. *Start and Run a Profitable Consulting Business: A Step-By-Step Business Plan.* Vancouver, British Columbia: Self Counsel Press, 1996.

Grissom, Fred, Steven Elias and David Pressman. *The Inventor's Notebook.* Berkeley, California: Nolo Press, 1996.

Hemphill, Barbara. *Kiplinger's Taming the Paper Tiger: Organizing the Paper in Your Life.* Washington, D.C.: Kiplinger Books, 1992.

Lonier, Terri, *The Frugal Entrepreneur: Creative Ways to Save Time, Energy and Money in Your Business.* New Paltz, New York; Portico Press, 1996

McGrath, Kate, and Stephen Elias. *Trademark: How to Name Your Business and Product.* Berkeley, California: Nolo Press,1996.

McKeever, Mike, *How to Write a Business Plan.* Berkley, California: Nolo Press, 1994.

Meyer, Jeffrey J., *If You Haven't Got Time to Do It Right, When Will You Find the Time to Do It Over?* New York: Fireside Books, 1990.

Mooney, Sean, *Insuring Your Business—What You Need to Know to Get the Best Insurance Coverage for Your Business.* New York: Insurance Information Institute Press, 7th ed., Harper Collins. 1992.

Nicholas, Ted. *How To Form Your Own S Corporation and Avoid Double Taxation.* Dover, New Hampshire: Upstart Publishing Co., 1995.

Pressman, David. *Patent It Yourself.* Berkeley, Calforina: Nolo Press,1997.

Pruissen, Catherine. *Start & Run a Profitable Home Daycare: Your Step-by-Step Business Plan.* Bellingham, Washington: Self-Counsel Press, 1993.

Ray, Norm, CPA, *Easy Financials for Your Home-Based Business: The Friendly Guide to Successful Management Systems for Busy Home Entrepreneurs.* Windsor, California: Rayve Productions Inc., 1992.

——— *Smart Tax Write-Offs: Hundreds of Tax Deduction Ideas for Home-Based Businesses, Independent Contractors and All Entrepreneurs.* Windsor, California: Rayve Productions Inc. 1996.

*Ready-to-Use Business Forms: A complete package for the small business.* Vancouver, British Columbia: Self-Counsel Business Series, 1992.

Small Business Association. *Business Plans for Small Manufacturers, Construction, Retail, Service and Home-Based Business.* Denver, Colorado: SBA Publications.

Steingold, Fred S. *The Legal Guide for Starting and Running a Small Business.* Berkeley, California: Nolo Press, 1997.

Touchie, Rodger. *Preparing a Successful Business Plan: A Practical Guide for Small Business*. Vancouver, British Columbia: Self-Counsel Business Series. 1993.

Whitmeyer, Claude: Salli Rasberry; and Michael Phillips. *Running a One-Person Business*. Berkeley, California: Ten Speed Press, 1994.

Winston, Stephanie. *Getting Organized*. Warner Books, New York, New York: 1991.

**CHAPTER FOUR**

Germer, Jerry. *The Complete Guide to Building and Outfitting an Office in Your Home*. Cincinnati, Ohio: Betterway Publications, 1994.

*Home Office Computing Magazine*, editors. *The Home Office Computing Handbook*, Blue Ridge Summit, Pennsylvania: Windcrest, 1994.

*Ideas for Great Home Offices*. Menlo Park, California: Sunset Books, 1995.

Kanarek, Lisa. *Organizing Your Home Office for Success—Expert Strategies That Can Work for You*. New York: NAL/Dutton (Plume), 1993.

King, Dean and Jessica. *Paper Clips to Printers: The Cost-Cutting Sourcebook for Your Home Office*. New York: Penguin USA, 1996.

Mack, Lorrie. *Making the Most of Work Spaces*. New York: Rizzoli International Publications, 1995.

Manroe, Candace Ord. *The Home Office: Setting Up, Furnishing and Decorating Your Own Workspace*. New York: Putnam Publishing Group, 1997.

Osborn, Hazel. *Room for Loving, Room for Learning: Finding the Space You Need in Your Family Child Care Home*. St. Paul, Minnesota: Redleaf Press, 1997.

Paul, Donna. *The Home Office Book*. New York: Artisan, 1996.

Reif, Daniel K. *Home Office-Small Office Quick Planner: Reusable, Peel-and-Stick Furniture and Architectural Symbols*. Chicago: Gardeners Guide, 1995.

*Setting Up for Infant Care: Guidelines for Centers and Family Day Care Homes*, edited by Annabelle Godwin. Washington DC: National Association for the Education of Young Children, 1988.

Shannon, Larry R. *Welcome to Home-Based Business Computing*. New York: MIS Press, 1995.

Skolnik, Lisa. *Home Offices*. New York: Friedman/Fairfax Publishing, 1996.

*The Ultimate Home Office: Designing, Planning and Creating the Perfect Workspace for Your Home or Apartment*. Alexandria, Virginia: Time-Life, 1997.

Vian, Kathi and Howard Bornstein. *Mac-World Home Office Companion*. New York: IDG Books Worldwide, 1996.

Zimmerman, Neal. *Home Office Design: Everything You Need to Know About Planning, Organizing and Furnishing Your Work Space*. New York: John Wiley & Sons, 1996.

## CHAPTER FIVE

Bly, Robert W. *Keeping Clients Satisfied— Make Your Service Business More Successful and Profitable*. New York: Prentice Hall, 1993.

———— *The Perfect Sales Piece: A Complete Do-It-Yourself Guide to Creating Brochures, Catalogs, Fliers and Pamphlets*. New York: John Wiley & Sons, 1994.

———— *Power-Packed Direct Mail: How to Get More Leads and Sales by Mail*. New York: John Wiley & Sons, 1996.

———— *Selling Your Services—Proven Strategies for Getting Clients to Hire You (or Your Firm)*. New York: Henry Holt & Co., 1991

Brabec, Barbara. *Handmade for Profit: Hundreds of Secrets to Success in Selling Arts & Crafts*. Cincinnati, Ohio: Betterway Publishing. 1996.

Brennan, Gregory. *Successfully Self-Employed*. Dover, New Hampshire: Upstart Publishing Co., 1996.

Brenner, Robert C. *Pricing Guide for Desktop Services: Street Smart Pricing for the Small Business Entrepreneur*. Chicago: Brenner Information Group, 1995.

Burgett, Gordon. *Sell & Resell Your Magazine Articles*. Cincinnati, Ohio: Writers Digest Books, 1997.

Crandall, Rick, *Marketing Your Services: For People Who HATE to Sell*. New York: Select Press, 1995.

Davidson, Jeffrey P. *Marketing on a Shoestring*. New York: John Wiley & Sons. 1994.

Dillehay, James. *The Basic Guide to Pricing Your Craftwork*. Torreon, New Mexico: Warm Snow Publishers 1997.

———— *The Basic Guide to Selling Arts & Crafts*. Torreon, New Mexico: Warm Snow Publishers, 1997.

Fletcher, Tana, and Julia Rockler. *Getting Publicity: A Do-It-Yourself Guide for Small Business and Non-Profit Groups*. Vancouver, British Columbia: Self-Counsel Press, 1995.

Floyd, Elaine. *Marketing With Newsletters*. St. Louis, Missouri: E.F. Communications, 1993.

Gordon, Kim T. *Growing Your Home-Based Business: A Complete Guide to Proven Sales & Marketing Strategies*. Englewood Cliffs, New Jersey: Prentice-Hall, 1994.

Gray, Douglas and Donald Cyr. *Marketing Your Product: A Planning Guide for Small Business*. Vancouver, British Columbia: Self-Counsel Press, 1994.

Harris, Godfrey. *How to Generate Word of Mouth Advertising: 101 Easy and Inexpensive Ways to Promote Your Business*. New York: Americas Group, 1995.

Husch, Tony, and Linda Foust. *That's a Great Idea-How to Get, Evaluate, Protect, Develop, and Sell New Product Ideas*. Berkeley, California: Ten Speed Press, 1990.

Levinson, Jay Conrad, Mark S.A. Smith and Orvel R. Wilson. *Guerrilla Trade Show Selling: New Unconventional Weapons and Tactics to Meet More People, Get More Leads and Close More Sales*. New York: John Wiley & Sons, 1997.

McIntyre, Catherine V. *Writing Effective News Releases-How to Get Free Publicity for Yourself; Your Business, or Your Organization*. New York: Piccadilly Books, 1992.

Phillips, Michael, and Salli Rasberry. *Marketing Without Advertising—Creative Strategies for Small Business Success*. Berkeley, California: Nolo Press, 1993.

Powers, Melvin. *Making Money with Classified Ads*. Los Angeles: Wilshire Books, 1995.

Schaefer, David. *Surefire Solutions for Growing Your Home-Based Business: Win More Clients, Charge What You're Worth, Collect What you're Owed and Get the Money You Need*. Chicago: Dearborn Trade, 1997.

Williams, Theo Stephan. *Pricing, Estimating & Budgeting (Graphic Design Basics)*. Cincinnati, Ohio: North Light Books, 1996.

# Index